Civil Justice After COVID

A Change for the Better?

An Examination of the Civil Justice System in England and Wales Pre and Post COVID 19 and the Impact on the Administration of Justice

ANTHONY REEVES

Emerald Guides

Emerald Guides

Copyright © Anthony Reeves 2021

Anthony Reeves has asserted the moral right to be identified as the author of this work.

All rights reserved. No part of this publication may be reproduced in a retrieval system or transmitted by any means, electronic or mechanical, photocopying or otherwise, without the prior permission of the copyright holders.

ISBN 978-1-913776-08-4
Printed by 4edge www.4edge.co.uk

Whilst every effort has been made to ensure that the information contained within this book is correct at the time of going to press, the author and publisher can take no responsibility for any errors or omissions contained within.

Contents

Introduction	1
1. The Courts Before COVID	7
2. We Are Not Accountants	27
3. Less Pre-Action, More Action	45
4. How Much to Reveal?	55
5. Remote Hearings	63
6. Changes to the Court Rules and Processes	75
7. Relief from Relief?	97
8. The Impact on Lawyers and their Clients	113
9. Funding the Civil Courts	125
Conclusion	137
Index	139

Introduction

This book does not intend to get all sociological about the purpose of the civil justice system. If you want to read about that then study a Jurisprudence course or something similar. The ordinary person may never use a civil court in their lifetime, but on the rare occasion they do, you might expect that they will have some romantic notion that the England & Wales courts are the envy of the world and something we should be proud of. After their first encounter, that rose-tinted view may well be dispelled when the reality of what it's really like hits home, and more painfully so if they lose.

"Civil Justice" can occupy many pages in books by legal scholars. In simple terms, civil justice is the process of how the law affects civil rights and duties and the machinery and resources provided by the state for the resolution of disputes between individuals and organisations. It comprises of the law, civil procedure, courts, and the judiciary. The challenge is to find a system that is reasonably accessible to enable people to enforce their rights and not be too complicated or expensive so that it discourages people from using the system. It boils down to how much civil justice can we afford? The criminal justice system has had a bigger share of the pie in terms of resources in the past couple of decades and the civil justice system is like the poor relation. This might be because crime is a social evil and there needs to be a suitable process for prosecuting offenders; it is also politically expedient to spend more money on addressing crime than helping people fight their battles in the civil courts.

People fighting battles is a narrow view of the purpose of having an effective civil justice system. It is not just so that the wealthy people can argue over what might seem trivial issues, but it goes hand in hand with a thriving economy. If businesses cannot enforce contracts or collect payments, then ultimately the economy will fail to survive in the modern world. A society which knows that it can escape its obligations or commitments because there is no system to force compliance, is living on borrowed time. It is also naive to think that we can all learn to settle our differences by being nicer people and never resort to legal action. Many years in legal practice has taught me that human beings are not always reasonable when it comes to resolving disputes. On the other hand, why should people have to compromise when they are in the right because the Ministry of Justice is trying to develop more schemes to prevent you becoming a court user. The Court Service is awash with all the right jargon and statements of what you can expect from service standards but, with the state of many courts, especially in the County Court, you do wonder what actual "service" is being provided. The Court Service must be a rare breed of organisation that can charge fees for providing services but can suffer little or no penalties if it provides no service.

The phrase "the world will never be the same again" is often used following a change in events. It is perhaps over used in response to events which might be important but are hardly world changing. COVID-19 is, however, widely

INTRODUCTION

viewed as one of those cases when this phrase is particularly apt. Probably nobody in living memory has experienced a pandemic that has caused a total lock down in society and has caused economic disaster.

The pandemic swept across the western world very quickly leaving politicians to make difficult decisions. The debate about what should have been done and when will no doubt rage on for many years and will exercise the thoughts of historians in the generations to come. Changes had to be made quickly to cope with the worsening situation and the emergency laws had to be brought in. The Courts faced a difficult time with measures needing to be introduced rapidly to avoid a total closure of court business. The COVID crisis has been disastrous for many people, but to the justice system it provided the catalyst to force the courts to embrace the modern digital world in respect of on-line court hearings. It is hoped that this shove in the direction of the modern world will continue in a post COVID world, and that it will not be a temporary experiment.

What will become apparent as you go through this book, is that you will see that there are more changes that are needed than simply better technology; a whole host of problems exist and some of the areas that need an overhaul are:

1. More resources for administrative staff and the appointment of more judges.
2. More streamlined procedures to enable a faster route to trial.
3. The abolition of costs budgeting.
4. Reform of certain procedures such as "relief from sanctions".

5. More straightforward disclosure rules.
6. Longer and more flexible court hours.
7. Fair and proportionate court fees.
8. The extension of fixed recoverable legal costs.
9. The relationship between client and lawyer.

Some of the ideas I put forward will be controversial. There is need for radical change. Too often we have reports which describe a vision for the future of the civil courts, but little happens. In the report by the Lord Chief Justice and the Senior President of Tribunals in September 2016 called "Transforming Our Justice System", the chapter on civil courts opened by saying:

> *Our ambition for the civil courts is that they retain and enhance their world-class position as the trusted jurisdiction of choice for international disputes, while becoming easier to use for everyone, and more proportionate in resolving simpler legal disputes. The system must work for everybody, from international trades with complex market disputes, companies filing claims in bulk, to the individuals filing one-off claims where they feel they have been wronged.*

It is debatable whether the vision of the courts "becoming easier to use for everyone" has been achieved. The section on civil courts continued:

> *Our reform will promote the full range of methods of settling disputes more swiftly, at less cost and with greater choice. This is likely to include a number of options, a dispassionate evaluation of the dispute, followed by negotiation, conciliation, mediation*

INTRODUCTION

or a tailored hearing to resolve the issues on which the parties remain in dispute. These options are designed to minimize combative hearings and help parties settle their disputes with the minimum of stress and acrimony, whether they are members of the public or multi-national corporations. Depending on the complexity of the case – and the needs of all involved – it might be online, paper-based or face-to-face.

We want to build on simpler consumer-focused models. In the civil courts, we will automate and digitize the entire process of civil money claims by 2020. These account for more than four fifths of the 1.6 million claims issued in the county courts and the High Court each year – with the vast majority (83%) of which are uncontested.

We will speed up resolution as we replace paper and post with digital working currently a 'fast track' claim with a value between £10,000-£25, 000 takes 11 months to be resolved'. Under our new digital model, cases will be handled faster and in a more convenient way, improving the experience for everyone making and defending claims in the civil courts.

More needs to be done to control the costs of civil cases so they are proportionate to the case, and legal costs are more certain from the start. Building on earlier reforms, we will look at options to extend fixed recoverable costs much more widely, so the costs of going to court will be clearer and more appropriate. Our aim is that losing parties should not be hit with disproportionately high legal costs, and people will be able to make more informed decisions on whether to take or defend legal action.

We also want to do more to make sure that if the court finds in your favour, you can get back what you are owed. We will *be extending the powers of the High Court, enabling them to make attachment of earnings orders so that debtors pay back their creditors. The County Court already has this power and this change will provide a further enforcement option for users in the High Court.*

There was little sign by 2020 of the new digital models apart from in the High Court where E-filing had been introduced. It has taken a global pandemic to adapt quickly to a new remote way of working. However, is this a reaction to the crisis or will it be a long-term change for the better?

Chapter 1

The Courts Before COVID

In late 2019 and early 2020, the County Courts were not in a healthy position. Years of staff reductions had led to long delays in cases being heard. There were many stories surfacing on the website "Civil Litigation Brief"[1] of county court hearings being cancelled at the very last minute through the non-availability of District Judges. Not only were cases being adjourned because of a lack of judges, the processing times for dealing with the issuing of claims and other court administration had grown to unacceptable levels. Some courts had more problems than others. There were courts in London that were listing small claims hearings up to 10 months ahead. For telephone hearings to happen, both parties usually had to have legal representation. There were many more cases that could have been dealt with by way of a telephone hearing, in particular the shorter applications that did not involve the hearing of witness evidence.

There was a sense that the County Courts were simply limping along with the prospect that the whole system was soon going to come to a grinding halt. The efficiency of some

---
[1] www.civillitigationbrief.com

of the County Courts in the metropolitan areas has long been a cause of concern. Certain courts, such as Central London County Court, have come in for serious criticism over the years and my recent experience of the Court does not fill me with enthusiasm. In 2005, Lord Justice Brooke in **CDC2020 v Ferreira [2005] EWCA Civ 611**, delivered a damming criticism of the administration at Central London County Court. Below is the extract from his judgment where he set out the facts of the delay and gave his stinging condemnation of the County Court:

"The judge gave judgment on 13th July 2004. On 2nd August the appellant's solicitors attempted to file a notice of appeal without seeking an extension of time. They thereupon set about obtaining the documents that needed to be filed for the purposes of the appeal. These included the order of Judge Rich QC and an approved transcript of his very short judgment. We have been told by the appellant's solicitor that he attended the Central London County Court personally in August and filled in the requisite forms.

When the court order and judgment transcript had not been forthcoming by 17th September, counsel advised him to ring the County Court enquiring about their whereabouts, which he duly did. On 3rd November, under heavy pressure from the Civil Appeals Office, he reported that he had been chasing the County Court for the court order and transcript to no avail, and that he was writing a further letter to them that day. On 4th November staff at the County Court asserted that they possessed no record showing that any party had asked for a transcript. Sadly, that court now has a bad reputation for misfiling documents and failing to record telephone messages. On 12th November the appellant's solicitor wrote to the County Court again requesting a transcript. By this time the County Court had at long last supplied him a copy of the court order, under cover of a letter dated 9th November. This had been completed and prepared for issue on 23rd August, over 11 weeks earlier. Nothing then happened. On 8th December he had to chase the County Court again. This elicited a letter written on 9th December acknowledging his letter written nearly four weeks earlier. The County Court then set about what he had asked them to do four months earlier.

A further delay now occurred while the transcribers were seeking and being paid a transcription fee before they were willing to start work. Eventually the very short transcript was sent to the judge for approval on 10th January, received back with amendments on 26th January, and filed on 2nd February 2005, six months after the first attempt to file the notice of appeal.

The problems besetting the Central London County Court are very well known to this court. There is a very high turnover of staff there each year and HM Court Service professes itself unable, with the resources currently provided to it, to correct the position to any significant extent. I am bound to say, however, that it is intolerable that litigants who pay the court fees required of them should be treated in this way. Despite the valiant efforts made by the staff and lawyers in the Civil Appeals Office to expedite matters, they were effectively thwarted by the non-availability of the judgment transcript so that it took six months before the papers could be placed before a Lord Justice to consider whether to grant permission to appeal.

In the meantime the marketing of this small residential development has been seriously prejudiced by the Central London County Court's delays. Because of the uncertainty arising from the fact that an appeal was pending, the developers were unable to market the three housing units for which the three garages had been erected. Since there was no stay on the judge's order they attempted to enforce that *part of it which obliged the appellant to remove the obstacles from the right of way at his own expense by 24th August 2004. These attempts, however, ran into the sand. Fortunately this court was able to offer a reasonably early date for the hearing of the appeal.*

I direct that a copy of this judgment be sent to the director within HM Court Service who is responsible for civil business in the London region and to the Master of the Rolls as head of Civil Justice. Somehow a way must be found of ensuring that the Central London County Court provides a service of the quality that litigants in that court and their legal advisers, and the staff, lawyers and judges of the Court of Appeal should be entitled to expect from those whose business it is to serve the courts and the members of the public who use them."

I do not think much has changed since 2005. From my own experience, many London County Courts still list claims way ahead, for example I had a small claims case that was started in October 2018 but did, not, receive a hearing until December 2019.

For years, the answers to increased demand were met with higher court fees and requirements to undertake greater pre-action protocol measures and to be persuaded to consider alternative methods of resolving disputes such as mediation. All it needed for the system to totally close was some major unforeseen event to happen-such as COVID-19.

The workload of the County Court
After the Woolf Reforms of 1999, the number of Civil cases issued in the County Court fell but started to rise again in 2006 to 2,157,000. The number fell away again by 2010 to 1,616,536. By 2018, the number of claims issued had risen to

2.07 million. The Annual Report from the Lord Chief Justice in November 2019 recorded the following in respect of the County Court:

> "Pressure on local civil justice continues to be acute. At County Court level challenges caused by shortages in civil judicial resources remain, worsening the adverse impact on the timescales of cases being determined and increasing pressure on frontline judiciary, despite the recruitment of significant numbers of Deputy District Judges. The numbers of County Court claims fell slightly in the second quarter of 2019 down 6% to 465,000 when compared to the same period in 2018."

As the workload has increased, the resources in terms of court staff have fallen as is shown below.

| **HM COURTS AND TRIBUNALS SERVICE STAFF** | | | | | |
| Annual average, England and Wales | | | | | |
Year	Permanently employed staff	Annual change (%)	Agency and contract staff	Annual change (%)	Total
2010/11	20,392	–	385	–	20,777
2011/12	19,433	–	271	–	19,704
2012/13	17,597	–	682	–	18,269
2013/14	16,999	-3%	830	22%	17,829
2014/15	16,162	-5%	871	5%	17.033
2015/16	15,209	-6%	1077	24%	16,286
2016/17	14,269	-6%	1480	37%	15,749
2017/18	13,841	-3%	2034	37%	15,875
2018/19	14,177	-2%	2042	0%	16,219

Source: HM Courts and Tribunals Service Annual Report and Accounts, Various Years

It is not surprising there are delays in the court process if the level of court staff has been reduced by about 4,500 from 2010 to 2019.

The increase in delays is shown by considering the average length of time it takes for a case to reach trial. In January to March 2019, it took an average of 36.9 weeks between a small claim being issued and the claim going to trial, 3.9 weeks longer than in the same period in the previous year. Since October to December 2016, where it stood at 30.4 weeks, the small claims mean time to reach trial has been increasing quarter on quarter. For January to March 2019, it is the longest mean time. For multi/fast track claims, it took on average 58.5 weeks to reach a trial, nearly 2 weeks longer than in January to March 2018.[2]

The listing of County Court cases
The listing of county court cases had always been a system that led to much waiting around.Indeed, in some cases, the hearing would not be heard, and the parties would be given another date several months ahead.

Listing in County Courts is usually by way of a block listing which means that the list might contain several cases at the same time. So, if you turn up for a small claims hearing listed for 10.am, you would find other small claims hearings listed to be heard at 10am. The court list might look as follows:

---

[2] Civil Justice Statistics Quarterly, England and Wales, January to March 2019.

THE COURTS BEFORE COVID

Before District Judge Jones sitting in Uptown County Court At 10am in Court room 1

Case No. F01RT123	Smith v. Jones	Small Claims Hearing – t/e 1 hour
Case No F02EF234	Bell v. Dobson	Small Claims Hearing – t/e 1 hour
Case No. GH09JN9	Dunn v. Steel	Small Claims hearing – t/e 2 hours

When you consider that the District Judge in the morning would sit from 10am until 1pm, it does not take a mathematical genius to work out that if all the cases are not settled and they require the full-time estimate, the cases are not going to be heard in the morning. That would mean that at least some of the listed cases would not be heard that morning unless the District Judge has a relatively short list in the afternoon, and he/she could finish off the case in the afternoon. If not, some of the parties who had been waiting around since 10am would be disappointed and must come back on another date. If the cases had not been small claims, but for example applications or fast track trials, more than likely it would have involved legal representatives attending and they would have wasted a whole morning in court; that would be an expense incurred by the client and probably not recoverable. To be fair to court listing officers, there are reasons for this kind of block listing. Cases will invariably settle leading up to a hearing and if the list were not block listed then court time would be under used. Some of the blame lies at the hands of the parties and legal representatives who do not tell the court as soon as the case settles. This prevents the court putting another case in the list because there is insufficient time to give the required notice to the parties.

Having sufficient time to re-allocate time to another case will of course also depend on the court staff dealing efficiently with correspondence. It is not unusual to receive Orders/letters from the court referring to matters several weeks previous; a District Judge may make an order relatively quickly after an application has been referred but it may be 4 to 5 weeks before the Order is sent out to the parties. It is probably due to a lack of administration staff in the courts. A lot of the County Court business in the issue of money claims has been centralised in the County Court Money Claims Centre in Salford, Manchester. When a claim is defended, it gets transferred to the home County Court hearing centre of the Defendant. Since 2013, all the local county courts are part of one unified "County Court", with each local court being a "hearing centre" of the "County Court". Before, you would have referred to the "XXX County Court", whereas now it is the "County Court at XXX". The difference is subtle, but it is supposed to recognise that there is one County Court. Many "local hearing centres" have their calls answered by a centralised call centre. It is difficult to contact many of the county courts by telephone. Speaking to a centralised call centre is not helpful when you have an urgent issue relating to an upcoming case; the call centre is not always in the same building as the court and so they will only have the information on their screen. In the old days, prior to 90 County Courts being closed, you could pick up the phone to your local county court and speak to the clerks, who if necessary, would pick up the file and answer your question or put it before the District Judge if something required urgent action. So, it is all very well for an Order to say things like *"please notify the court immediately a case is settled"*, but even if you do, your correspondence may go to some centralised admin centre or a general e-mail address with the processing time being too long.

4. Courts and court closures by area
Since 2010, the court and tribunal estate has changed significantly. Based on the available information, between 2010 and 2019

- **162 magistrates' courts** *have closed, out of 323.*
- **90 county courts** *have closed, out of 240.*
- **18 dedicated tribunal buildings** *have closed out of 83.*
- **17 family courts** *have closed out of 185.*
- **8 crown courts** *have closed, out of 92.*

In total 295 court facilities (the individual services listed above) closed during this time.

These numbers may not tally with those reported elsewhere because some sources count the closure of premises and others count the closure of service in given location.

(Source: this is an extract from "Court statistics for England and Wales", Briefing Paper 16 December 2019, House of Commons Library, by Georgina Sturge").

The reasons for closing many county courts and centralising the issuing of money claims in Salford was to achieve savings through economies of scale. In addition to the closure of many local county courts, admin staff was reduced by a third.

The centralisation of civil justice has not improved efficiency and it has made the County Court the poor relation to the High Court. Not only have there been cutbacks and delays to the court user, but court fees have steadily increased since the introduction of the Woolf reforms in 1999. The reforms of Lord Woolf saw the introduction of a new set of civil procedure rules which were heralded as a shorter and more straightforward set of procedures; the overriding duty was for civil cases to be dealt with fairly, expeditiously and at proportionate cost. Many would say that the objectives of Woolf have not been achieved but that is not the fault of Lord Woolf. The objectives of the reforms were right but somewhere in the last 15 years or so the Ministry of Justice and other bodies that contribute to the civil justice system have not kept to the objectives of Woolf. The reality is that governments have meddled for reasons of policy to cut back on the cost of the civil courts. What we are left with is a County Court system that is in intensive care desperately trying to function.

Some of the blame for poor use of court time and delays rests with lawyers. It is well known that if you give a longer time estimate, the chances are that you will have to wait longer for a hearing date. However, that approach does backfire. It will invariably lead to an adjournment because a District Judge in a busy list which does not run to schedule, will pick up an application for the first time (for example an application summary judgment which has been listed for one hour) and must decide whether the remaining 45 mins of the morning list is sufficient to even make a start. It could possibly be dealt with if everything went to plan and the other side had not filed shed loads of pointless witness statements in reply, but mostly the Judge will take the cautious approach and adjourn it. It will probably be adjourned with a longer time estimate of say two hours and that will take several more months to find a slot in the list. However, the key reason for lengthy delays is the fact that the courts (especially the County Court) do not have the resources to meet the demand. It was telling that during the first COVID lockdown, the Government decided to open "Nightingale Courts" to deal with the backlog of cases. A shame that many of the suitable County Court buildings that were closed had been sold for development. For example, Chippenham County Court had only been opened in 1997 and was closed in 2018. It was a purpose-built modern Court which housed the County Court and the local Magistrates Courts.

The decision to close 90 County Courts and centralise civil justice goes against the idea of local justice. Many individuals, for example defendants in housing cases, must travel a long way to attend possession hearings. In rural areas, a lack of public transport or nearby parking makes the journey a difficult one, especially for those on low incomes. Not only are journeys more difficult for those needing to attend court, but it goes against the policy of reducing travel to decrease the impact of pollution and the carbon footprint.

Before COVID, the civil court lists were being taken up by too many matters that are a waste of court time. There appears to be too much time taken up with case management and controlling costs. Should District Judges in the County Court and Masters in the High Court be using court hearing time to decide whether a costs budget is proportionate? As will be discussed later, costs budgets are a requirement in larger multi-track cases. Ironically, it is the excessive case management that adds quite considerably to legal costs because of the costs of preparing for such a hearing and the instructing of Counsel to attend.

There have been proposals before to extend fixed costs. The report entitled "Transforming Our Justice System", by the Lord Chancellor, the Lord Chief Justice and the Senior President of Tribunals, was published in September 2016. There was some opposition. The Law Society was against the idea stating that these plans are 'totally inappropriate' as limiting recoverable costs on more complex cases would threaten access to justice. It stated that:

> *'...fixed costs for higher value claims can be prejudicial and disproportionately disadvantage those on lower incomes and the vulnerable'.*

In my view, this stance reflects a defending of a vested interest, especially those larger city firms who engage in what I call "cost churning".

The reality is that if fixed costs were brought into higher value claims it would affect how large firms operate. If the paying client knew that if he won, he would only recover £X from the loser, then there would be a trend toward the client not expecting to be charged more than what can be recovered. In theory, this should create pressure from clients for a reduction in legal costs as more firms enter the market providing proportionate costs. Obviously, some clients will be quite prepared to pay more than what they are permitted to recover but it would put downward pressure on legal fees. It is usually the larger city firms that charge higher rates. I have been involved in cases involving a claim for £100,000 where the defending solicitors prepare a costs budget for more than double the amount claimed. The case was not especially complex. It is the structure of larger firms and the desire to have a team of lawyers on the case that leads to these ridiculous cost budgets. These cases would probably be headed up by a "Partner", then an "Associate Solicitor" and a "Trainee Solicitor", plus the administrative back up. They would also involve Counsel in the case. In the larger firms, the Partner would have overall charge of the matter, but the reality is that the others do the work, and he/she signs it off. Does it benefit the client? Well, the service is often regarded as being less personal in that if the client wanted to discuss the case, it is unlikely they would be able to easily speak with the "Partner". Some of the cost budgets produced by these firms in litigation make your eyes water and question how they could spend so much time on some aspects of the case.

The **"Transforming Our Justice System"** report of September 2016 described making civil justice more digitalised. The reality was that before COVID the County Courts were far from being electronic. The Chancery and Queens Bench Divisions of the High Court were certainly fully digitalised. Issuing a claim in the High Court is such an easy process compared to the County Court. A claim over £100,000 in the County Court cannot not be issued on-line. Even the Money Claims Online system (which can be used for claims up to £100,000) is not adequate. You can serve separate particulars of claim but there is a danger that when you file the separate particulars of claim within 14 days, they may not be matched up with the online claim.

The Civil Courts (and especially the County Courts) are plagued by several problems. Before the COVID pandemic came along in March 2020, it was becoming more frustrating to the court user, and lawyers alike. It was like an older computer struggling to start up and when it did, it would experience a total freeze up so nothing could be done. The start of the current demise came with the centralisation of money claims in 2012. All money claims that are not commenced through Money Claims Online must be processed at the County Court Money Claims Centre. The reason I say this was a step in the wrong direction is that it meant that money claims could no longer be issued in your local County Court. The advantage of issuing in your local Court was that it appeared to be much more efficient and it was possible to speak directly to the clerks in the Court office to find out the state of affairs in a particular case. You got to know the local Court staff quite well; if needed, you could attend in person at the Court office counter. Court claims issued in your local County Court would in most cases take a week to ten days at most. In some more efficient smaller Courts, the papers would be processed almost by return. Although there were some notoriously inefficient Courts, such as Central London County Court, you got the impression that the Court staff cared about what they did.

The introduction of the County Court Money Claims Centre coincided with the closure of many County Courts. Administration at local courts has been drastically reduced and now all the local County Courts (the ones that are left) are known as "hearing centres". Each local hearing centre has a lot fewer admin staff, and, in many areas, the answering of telephones has been centralised in call centres that do not have access to the files. They are only able to see notes on the system about the general progress of a case, such as being able to see that a document was received on such a date if it has been logged on the system. When you phone a court, you usually spend the first 5 minutes being told (by a recorded message) that you can speak in another language if you like and details of where to find their data protection policy, before being told that there is zero tolerance to anyone showing any signs of not being politically correct or asking a perfectly sensible question.

If a claim is issued through the CCMC, then the volume of work means that it can often take 3 to 4 weeks before the matter is processed and served on the Defendant. If you try to contact the CCMC, then do not expect to be able to get through on the phone without a long wait. If you e-mail the Court, you receive auto responses setting out the expected response times. It does not really matter if it says, within '10 working days' or '10 weeks" as often you do not receive a reply; if you do get a reply, you get some form of stock answer. Later, when you receive an auto-response which says *deleted – not read*', I wonder if many e-mails get read or given any real attention. I have these visions, especially in lockdown, of court clerks working from home on their laptop dealing with enquiries in between watching daytime television. I expect the reason why the phones are not being answered is they are taking part in a phone-in on ITV's "This Morning" about stress at work.

One of the stock answers you are given if you get through on the phone is that the matter has been referred to the District Judge. When I enquired once as to how long it might take to receive a reply, I was told that as the Judges are working remotely, the court files must be delivered to the Judges and then returned to the court for typing. In this digital age, surely it would cheaper to buy a few scanners so that paperwork for the judges can be sent by e-mail which would be much more efficient. With this large-scale referring to Judges, it makes me wonder whether the admin staff are able or can process anything without it being referred to a Judge. Again, this is a sign of too much case management. I may be mistaken, but in days gone by the Court staff had a listing officer who would deal with most things concerning the listing of an application or hearing and they had good knowledge and experience of how long a particular application would take and therefore how many matters they could put in the list. However, where lawyers are representing parties, they are required to state a time estimate when making an application. Although lawyers do not always get their time estimates accurate, it ought to be a good basis on which to list the application and so I can never see the need to always refer to a Judge for listing. If all this referring to District Judges over matters could be dealt with better by trained and better qualified Court staff, it would speed up the administration process.

Not much has changed to the Money Claims Online System since it was implemented in 2002. It is good for simple unpaid debts. The space for entering the particulars of claim is limited; you can serve separate particulars of claim within 14 days of the claim being served but the separate particulars of claim are filed at Court in paper form. There is a danger that they do not get linked up to the file. A simple method of uploading the particulars of claim is required. Such an E-filing system exists for the High Courts.

Issuing a claim through the High Court E-filing system is an absolute breeze. I have uploaded a new claim on a Saturday afternoon and 15 minutes later the claim form was issued and returned ready for me to serve. Admittedly there may be fewer cases in the High Court compared to the County Court, but it is efficient and user friendly.

Of course, there is one major difference between the County Court and High Court in that the High Court requires the party/legal representative to serve the claim on the Defendant. This is something which needs to be applied to the County Court and is something that is considered in more detail later.

No doubt the E-filing system for the High Court has had more resources invested in it. There was a big increase in High Court fees in 2014 and perhaps some of that has gone towards this. Also, foreign businesses like to use the jurisdiction of England and Wales and so these wealthy individuals using the High Court in London undoubtedly generate revenue. Claims over £10,000 attract a Court fee of 5% of the amount claimed up to a maximum of £10,000. A claim for more than £100,000 can be issued in the High Court. The focusing of resources on the bigger High Court cases attracts a greater return and adds to the belief that the Civil Courts are there to serve the rich.

Where a claim in either the CCMC or the Money Claims Online is defended, the County Court will transfer it to the appropriate County Court Hearing Centre. If the Defendant is an individual, that will be his local County Court; if the Defendant is a company, then that will most likely be the preferred hearing centre of the Claimant. If the Claimant has legal representatives, then that will be the Court local to their lawyers.

It does not take a genius to realise that this transfer can cause a further delay. When the local Court receives the file, it then must consider what directions are appropriate. It will be referred to the District Judge to give those directions. With each of the local County Courts having limited admin resources, you can understand why it takes a while for the directions to be typed up and sent out. As I said before, some of the local Courts are grouped together so that their phones and administration is done by a central office. For example, Brighton will deal with the admin for the neighbouring Courts in the region. There are still some Courts that deal with their own admin and answer their own phones such as Portsmouth, but the numbers are dwindling.

What is then likely to happen is that a small claims track case (which are cases not exceeding £10,000) will be allocated a hearing date that will probably be several months down the line. A small claims track case has fewer formal procedures and a general rule of legal costs not being awarded. When you read internet blogs and other items from non-lawyers it will be said that this encourages lawyers to not be involved or lawyers do not need to be instructed. That is true but with the massive increase in small claims (perhaps caused to a degree by Joe Bloggs being told how straightforward it is), courts are inundated with claims that have not been properly prepared by the lay person or claims that do not even have a proper cause of action. This is a great waste of Court time and a strong argument for some fixed costs in the small claims track. Having a small, fixed, amount for legal costs in the small claims track would encourage litigants in person to get at least some basic advice.

Claims above £10,000 (but which do not exceed £25,000)

are usually allocated to the fast-track. A series of standard directions are issued which will normally include, disclosure, witness statements and expert evidence if needed. Fast-track cases are supposed to be listed in a trial window which is aimed to happen about 26 weeks after allocation to the fast-track. What usually happens with the listing of fast-track trials is that a County Court Hearing Centre will have days of the month when they list fast track trials.

The Court will usually list several cases for the same day. This will happen for small claims but also fast-track cases. The Court works on the basis that several of the cases will settle and so there will be time to hear the remaining unsettled cases. In my experience, the Court listing section leaves it quite late before the fast-track or small claims track is due to be heard to see if the case will proceed. If all the cases on the list have not settled, then there is a late scramble to see if the case can be heard at a nearby County Court. The problem being that there will often be a difficulty in finding a Judge at short notice. The inevitable result is the case is adjourned and so much for the matter being in the so called 'fast-track'.

It is probably easier for Courts to fit in several small claims into the list, even if there is limited time. A small claims hearing does not usually follow a formal procedure and the District Judge has the power under CPR Part 27 to conduct the hearing as he thinks fit. If there is a bit of time pressure the District Judge may take control of proceedings and rather than have formal evidence from witnesses, he/she might elicit the relevant facts by asking the parties a series of questions. Once the facts are established, the District Judge can apply any points of law and then move to giving a decision with limited reasons. It might be described as somewhat arbitrary justice but the Court rules regard cases of a value of up to £10,000 as being 'small'. £10,000 might not be small in the eyes of some litigants but the overruling objective of the civil rules is to allocate a proportionate amount of time and resources to a case.

If a case of small monetary value was of such legal significance or so complex in nature, then it is open for the parties to argue on the Directions Questionnaire for the case to be allocated to the fast-track or the multi-track.

Before COVID, small claims hearings were not conducted by telephone or video link, and it was rare for cases to be decided on the papers. As most cases that a District Judge deals with are small claims, perhaps too much in the way of resources are being allocated to such cases. A monetary claim over £25,000 or certain types of claims are allocated to the 'multi-track'. It is the multi-track that has many more procedural steps to be followed before a trial is reached. It can often take up to 2 years from the date a claim is allocated to it getting to trial. If the hearing of a case lasts more than a day, then it cannot proceed in the fast track and will be allocated to the multi-track. What can often happen is that legal representatives mistakenly believe that witness evidence will take longer than it should. On the other hand, it might be a tactic of the litigation to push it into the multi-track to put pressure on the other side who may get concerned that the level of costs will be too high and so decide to settle. It might also be a result of lawyers not being able to prepare witness statements that properly address the key issues and calling for too many unnecessary witnesses.

A case that is allocated to the multi-track will go through the following steps.

1. The Directions Questionnaire will need to be completed and returned with:
   a. Disclosure Report
   b. Costs Budget
   c. Budget Report
   d. Draft Directions

A cost and case management conference will then be listed at which the costs budgets will be considered, and directions given if the parties have not managed to agree them. The directions given will then usually be as follows, with variations for different types of cases:

- Disclosure
- Inspection
- Witness Statements
- Instruction of an expert (if needed)
- Questions to experts
- Pre-trial review
- Filing of pre-trial check lists
- Preparation for the trial
- The trial.

In addition to the above, the parties are expected to engage in settlement discussions, or some form of Alternative Dispute Resolution such as Mediation. If you add in the cost of complying with all the pre-Court action protocols, which can be quite lengthy, it is easy to understand how the costs of a multi-track can start to escalate.

SUMMARY

Before the onset of COVID, the Civil Justice system was not in a good state of health. There had been a marked decline in the number of Court Service staff and the times taken to reach a trial had on average increased in the small claims track, fast track and multi-track. Despite efforts to recruit more Deputy District Judges in the County Court, there were a lot of incidences of trials being adjourned because of a lack of judges.

Chapter 2

We Are Not Accountants

One of the most obvious changes that needs to be made to civil procedure post COVID is the removal of "Costs Budgeting". Since it was introduced in 2013, it has divided the legal profession and I can only believe it has survived due to vested interests which stand to lose a great deal if it were abolished. There is certainly no logical argument for costs budgeting in lower value cases and I look forward to the implementation of Lord Jackson's desire to introduce fixed costs for multi-track cases of up to £250,000. If cost budgeting is to remain, then it should only be used in high value litigation.

To the ordinary client who has no previous experience of civil litigation, the idea of cost budgeting may seem a sensible idea which is of great benefit to them. They think that it will keep costs down and they will know what costs they are risking in the litigation. The downside of cost budgeting is not often in my experience put forward by the legal profession, or if it is, then the comments are anonymous in the comment sections on the Law Society Gazette website. One can understand legal practitioners not wanting to put their head above water on issues for fear of the consequences; there are some very persuasive arguments that have been put forward by barristers in the costs field who make a good case for abolishing this pointless exercise. One of the most interesting articles I have read was the presentation by barrister Andrew Hogan to the Law Society in 2017.[3] It questioned the usefulness of costs budgeting.

Before going on to examine the case for Costs Budgeting, let us explore in simple terms what it is. It was introduced in April 2013 and stemmed from evidence that costs were getting out of control in litigation and was designed to give the parties an idea of the risk they faced in terms of paying the other side's costs if the case was lost. The process of costs budgeting does not apply to all cases. It applies generally to cases that are to be allocated to the Multi-Track, which is usually the more complex cases having a value of more than £25,000 with a trial time of more than a day. When a defence is filed, the court sends out a notice of allocation and the directions questionnaire to complete. Where the case is expected to be suitable for the multi-track, the court will list a "Costs and Case Management Conference" (CCMC) which will usually last from one hour to 90 minutes. The parties must complete "Precedent H". If the case is not worth more than £50,000, only the front page needs to be completed. A litigant in person does not need to complete a costs budget.

As can be seen from Precedent H, it is divided into "Incurred costs" and "Estimated costs". The case is then broken down into various stages. The guidance notes that

---

[3] October 2017 – Law Society Commercial Litigation Conference in Chancery Lane on the subject of costs budgeting.

go with the form explain what should be put in each section. To be able to put an accurate figure in the "incurred costs" section, this requires the lawyer to have time recording. There is legal software on the market which offers case management and time recording. I have always regarded time recording as being an irritating (but sometimes necessary) activity. As a trainee, I recall that trying to get your time sheet up to the required hours was a source of great anxiety. John Grisham's legal thrillers have often mocked how large law firms seem to bill more hours in a day than exist. However, as was pointed out to me at a costs conference several years ago, when assessing what are proportionate costs, regard should be had to various factors including the importance of the matter and how complex it is.

It is a requirement to file a Costs Budget by the required date otherwise there is the draconian sanction that the party failing to do so will only be able to claim court costs and no legal costs at all. If the deadline is missed, an application for relief from the sanction can be made but there is of course no guarantee that the application will be granted. The fear of missing a costs budget deadline is the nightmare of every civil litigator. The applications for relief from sanctions have become another area of contention in that in seeking to ensure compliance with rules, it has created satellite litigation and run up further costs as well as using up valuable court time. The winner out of the many applications for relief from sanctions is the Courts and Tribunal Service which collects a nice little fee for each application. A cynic would say that this was the reason for introducing a crackdown on compliance with rules and then requiring an application for relief from sanction. I return to this subject later in the book.

The presentation by Andrew Logan sets out the shortfalls with costs budgeting:

Costs budgeting and evidence

19. So when evaluating the benefits of costs budgeting and costs management more generally it might be thought logical to consider whether this rule change has worked to reduce costs, from disproportionate levels to proportionate levels and to consider how much the rule change itself has cost in terms of transactional or frictional costs.

20. This latter consideration could be looked at narrowly in terms of the costs of drawing up budgets, negotiating the attending costs management hearings and the ongoing process of review of costs: "that costs of the costs". Alternatively it could consider costs more widely in terms of the effect of any delays created by the process the knock-on consequence for higher litigation costs overall and perhaps wider economic benefits and dis-benefits.

What the above argues is that there has not been sufficient consideration of whether the introduction of costs budgeting has achieved one of the objectives of making costs more proportionate. Was sufficient consideration taken of the actual costs of arguing about costs? Is it really good use of scarce court time to have lengthy hearings to argue about whether the amount to be spent on preparing witness statements is too much? The reality is the client could not give a toss and what they will keep asking their lawyer is when is the court going to decide the issues in dispute. The average client finds it strange that in a system where the parties will wait a long time (up to 2 years in many bigger cases) to arrive at a trial, the court thinks it is fine to waste time arguing over costs. All the client wants to know from his lawyer is: Will I win? When is the trial? Will I recover my costs? Many clients wonder why they must incur costs in preparing a budget so that the court can decide how much they can spend. They do not like another obstacle in the way of getting a decision in a case. Also, this additional obstacle involves the client spending more money, such as to instruct Counsel to attend the CCMC if the cost issues and directions are not agreed. A failure to file a costs budget can lead to severe costs penalties; the logic of encouraging litigants to not spend unnecessary costs on legal action is made rather ironic by the fact that if they fail to spend the money to get the costs budget filed properly, they are at risk of not being able to recover their legal costs.

Of course, the supporters of costs management say that matters can be agreed beforehand but the lead up to a CCMC can become a bit of pointless psychological warfare; you will have the big city practices trying to scare the living daylights out of their smaller opponents by producing an excessive costs budget. The small firm will then, and this is not always understood by clients or lawyers, present what is seen as a budget that is too low and will be criticised for not being a realistic amount of costs they are spending on the case. The reality may be that the small firm has produced a realistic estimate of costs and not built in too many contingencies that have less chance of happening than the Pope becoming Protestant.

A reasonable costs budget could indicate that the person handling the litigation knows what he is doing and what the case is all about rather than going on an expedition with no map indicating where he is going. It may be a cynical view but some of the excessive costs budgets simply reflect that law firms want to make profits, as do other businesses. Nothing wrong with making profits as every business needs money to function, but unless the structure or culture that creates this desire to put down silly amounts of hours on a costs budget, then we are still going to be wasting court time arguing over whether a grade A fee earner should spend "X" number of hours on a particular stage of the case.

The more experienced client will understand that costs budgeting is like other attempts by the Court Service to hide the fact that there is a lack of resources to do what it should be doing, which is allowing the courts to decide disputes and not carrying out an accounting exercise in deciding what is proportionate or not. Other measures that are in this category include the heavy pressure on parties to mediate.

Further on in the presentation of Andrew Hogan, he raises the other pertinent points against costs budgeting:

22. Moreover there was little sense of scale in the paper given that we know that the majority of cases or claims settle without issue, that of those that are issued the vast majority settle before trial, and yet the costs budgets requirement was imposed in every case on the multi-track requiring the expenditure of resources to produce cost budgets and to comply with the costs management rules on the basis of scenario which will never come to pass: that all cases will go to trial.

As the Court Service and the Civil Procedure Rules emphasize that the parties to an action should take steps to avoid a trial, it is therefore not often that cases will go to a full trial and so all the time and expense in preparing a costs budget is wasted. In lectures in 2015, the Master of the Rolls stated that no business person would embark upon a project without having prepared a budget. That might be the case but the difference as I see it between general business budgets and costs budget in litigation, is that you can spend more money in commercial situations if you can fund it but in a court costs budget scenario you are seeking the approval of the court. The reality is the individual may well spend more than the approved costs budget but is not going to be able recover more than the figure in the costs budget. The argument for a costs budget is that you will have an idea of what your opponent will be claiming from you if you lost the case. This could also be achieved if there were fixed costs and would avoid the time and expense of preparing a costs budget.

Not only is there division as to the usefulness of costs budgeting, but the actual process itself is flawed. A good example is the fact that incurred costs are not up for consideration at the Cost Management hearing although the Judge can make comments on these items. The consequence of this is that lawyers will attempt to front load a large proportion of their costs into the "incurred" section so that it cannot be considered at the case management conference without good reason. **(Harrison v University Hospitals and Coventry and Warwickshire NHS Trust [2017] EWCA Civ 792).** Comments on the incurred costs can be made by the Judge conducting the CCMC so that they can be considered at a detailed assessment, but the Court should only depart from the Costs budget if there is good reason to do so. This exposes the flaw in the process of cost budgeting and therefore why spend so much judicial time on it.

In practice, with a party that has a disproportionate amount of incurred costs, the CCMC Judge could decide that the costs budget overall is disproportionate and therefore would not be able to have all the estimated costs section included in its budget. For example, let us say that a Claimant is pursuing a claim that is worth £90,000. If a costs budget were presented with £50,000 in the incurred costs stages and the overall budget was £125,000, it might be said that the costs budget was disproportionate. However, there are other factors to consider in deciding if a costs budget is disproportionate. You might also consider the complexity of the case and the importance of the issue to the parties. The claim might not be in value terms at the dizzy heights of some cases that are litigated in the High Court, but it could involve a novel or complex point of law or facts. Nonetheless, if the court were to decide that a proportionate costs budget for this claim of £90,000 was in the region of £85,000, then the party would not have a great deal of budget left for future costs. But does that really matter? The answer is "no" in the sense that a party can spend as much as it likes on a case but costs budgets deal with what costs are recoverable. This point was made clear by Mr Justice Birss in **Red and White Services Ltd v Phil Anslow Ltd & Anor [2018] EWHC 1699 (Ch)** when he said:

> "Costs budgeting is not directly concerned with how much a party can actually spend to protect their reputation either. Wealthy litigants can spend what they like but whether they can recover what they spend from the other party is a different matter. The budget is concerned with recoverable costs."

WE ARE NOT ACCOUNTANTS

In my mind, the fact that you can spend what you like but you will not be able to recover more than your costs budget except for a good reason, supports the view that the whole process of cost budgeting is a big waste of court time. Further, as Andrew Hogan described in the presentation to the Law Society because courts have moved to spending less time agonising over costs matters, then why not simply have fixed costs? Fixed costs are said to be unfair because the level of the fixed costs might be set at rather arbitrary levels, but that is happening anyway when it comes to courts considering costs:

69. In years gone by, I recall undertaking detailed assessments lasting three days, where a bill of costs was more than £150,000. Last year, I undertook a summary assessment of a schedule of costs claiming £140,000 in the Commercial Court, where the costs were assessed within 15 minutes. As is well known, on a provisional assessment of a bill of costs of up to £75,000, the court service allows a costs judge only 40 minutes.

70. The point is that, a philosophical shift has been adopted by the judges, that rather than spend days or even hours, agonizing over a claim for costs they will administer "rough justice" when making decisions.

I have not heard a convincing argument to retain costs budgeting and cannot understand the delay in moving towards fixed costs, certainly at the lower end of the scale in multi-track cases. Lord Jackson in his report several years ago argued for the moving to fixed costs for claims up to £250,000 but this has stalled after the consultation process. There must be a stronger vested interest resisting the move; I have seen changes made much more quickly on extraordinarily little consultation (such as court fee increases). I recall attending a costs seminar promoted by one of the large law costs firms and put this point to the District Judge who now edits "Cook on Costs" [regarded as the bible on Costs issues]. The rather abrupt answer was that costs budgeting should not take long if it is done properly. I wonder whether the reasons that few people seem to do it properly, or rather the large amount of case law that has developed with criticisms of costs budgets, could suggest that the whole process is flawed. One can understand vested interests protecting their field, and to move over to fixed costs would put many costs draftsmen out of business, but is it right for the unsatisfactory status quo to remain because of the dithering that is happening to remove this bulging area of satellite litigation?

Another point which is often overlooked regarding costs budgeting is that most cases will settle before trial. A comment on the Law Society Gazette website in response to an article on Lord Woolf speaking to Bond Solon's expert witness conference in November 2019 about the fact that costs are still high, summed up this point perfectly:

"I would estimate that I have drafted over 400 cost budgets. Not a single one of these cases went to trial, and the budgets were of no use whatsoever. At a cost of around £750 per client for drafting this, and another £2,000 or so for counsel to attend a CCMC, that is over £1.1 million in costs, much of which is wasted as in most cases directions can be agreed without the need for any court hearing.

WE ARE NOT ACCOUNTANTS

Costs budgeting has a place in complex litigation – it is a complete waste in straightforward contract claims."

Comments left on the Law Society Gazette website are often anonymous and controversial. However, they are comments from lawyers at the coal face of legal practice and comments left in this way is perhaps the only way to get a true picture of what the profession thinks about reforms and changes to the civil procedure rules.

As this book was being prepared for publication, a member of the judiciary bravely spoke out against costs budgets. Master Davison, in the case of **Patricia Smith v. W Ford & Sons (Contractors) Ltd [2021] EWHC 1749 (QB)**, said:

"I would make several observations about that. The first is that these factors were considered corporately by the Asbestos Masters and by the senior judiciary who devised the present system and approved the convention that costs budgeting should not usually apply. The factors that are generally in favour of costs budgeting were judged to be subordinate to the factors that I have mentioned. I would make two further observations, which are related. The first is that there is no evidence that the process of detailed assessment is not adequately controlling costs in asbestos cases. If the costs of asbestos cases were placed against the costs incurred in other cases of industrial disease, which have been costs budgeted, I would be surprised if there were much, if indeed any, difference. At any rate, if a defendant wishes to displace an important and well-established convention, then it seems to me that it is for that defendant to show, rather than merely assert, that costs in asbestos cases are disproportionate or not adequately controlled. Secondly, QB Masters, Chancery

> *Masters and Costs Judges do not necessarily share this defendant's expressed confidence that costs budgeting controls costs better, or more effectively, than detailed assessment. This is a large topic and a complex and somewhat sensitive issue. The present hearing is not, perhaps, the forum to debate it at any length. Suffice it to say that I do not agree with the Defendant's characterisation of this case as presenting a dichotomy between the tight control of costs on the one hand and a free-for-all on the other. That is, in my view, inaccurate".*

It is quite clear from this judgment of Master Davison that costs budgeting clogs up the courts and is a waste of time.

There is much debate as to whether it was the Woolf reforms which have brought about the chaos that now exists, especially in the County Court. Some say that the Woolf reforms with its support of case management and front loading of costs with pre-action protocols, has increased costs at the start of a case whereas others would say that the changes introduced in the past 10 years or so have not reflected Woolf's true intention. As always, such matters are not always so black and white and the reason for the difficult state of the civil courts is a combination of factors. I take the view that the changes that have been made, such as big increases in court fees, increased case management, costs budgeting, an ever-growing list of pre-action protocols, a stronger pressure on parties to use ADR and the increase in regulation of lawyers, were policy decisions from the Ministry of Justice, some to cut costs and others in a misguided belief that it would benefit the court user.

Some of the ever-expanding table of Civil Procedure Rules with amendments being introduced frequently is not a measure that would have been anticipated by Lord Woolf in the early days after his reforms were implemented. Much of the avalanche of change could be linked to interference with a system by advisers and policy makers who believe that they need to tinker around with the process and at the same time hope it will save the Ministry of Justice some money. The problem is that those "consultants" or "advisers" who oversee making reforms often do not have sufficient experience of the legal system.

The key issue with the Civil Procedure Rules is that they have grown like an out-of-control wildfire. There are (as of September 2020) 89 Civil Procedure Rules with each rule having practice directions, with more than one in some cases. In October 2020, the 120th Amendment to the civil procedure rules was implemented. These updates come more frequently than new car registrations. There are another 14 assorted practice directions ranging from Insolvency Proceedings to County Court Closures! When the Woolf Reforms were introduced in April 1999, there were only 40 civil procedure rules. I recall hearing Lord Woolf speak in 1999 and he said he wanted to have a concise set of rules that would fit on his bed side table. He now needs a large bed-side table before it collapses under the weight of new Rules and Amendments.

SUMMARY

Costs budgeting is a perfect example of a process that has little benefit to the court user and only serves to waste valuable judge time having to decide issues they should not be involved in. The issue of disproportionate costs has largely arisen because some lawyers have engaged in cost churning and claiming an unreasonable amount in costs. The courts sought to control escalating costs and believed that cost budgeting would curb the excesses. The problem is that it has created satellite litigation and wasted court time arguing over what is disproportionate.

A large contingent in the legal profession find cost budgeting most irritating and clients incur more costs participating in this pointless exercise. The solution is for wider fixed costs and a simple summary assessment at the end of a hearing where the judge makes a broad-brush evaluation as to what figure is reasonable for costs.

Costs budgeting is a classic example of where there is a problem it is always assumed that there needs to be a complicated solution. In this case, the solution is worse than the mischief it was designed to cure. A quick summary assessment may seem arbitrary and a little harsh but is in keeping with the overriding objective of deploying an appropriate amount of court resources to a case.

Costs draftsman will feel outraged by the reduction in their work, but we want lawyers and judges to be lawyers and not accountants.

WE ARE NOT ACCOUNTANTS

Chapter 3

Less Pre-Action, More Action

In the old days, before the Woolf reforms, the extent of pre-action communication often consisted of a letter giving notice of legal action within 7 days, with little detail about the claim. I am not advocating a return to a system of not revealing any information, but the current extent of pre-action protocols has spread like Japanese Knotweed. I glibly mention "before Woolf" as if he is a god-like figure because he was the person that undertook a review of civil procedure that changed it for the better. The changes were certainly significant, and it was big news in its day, but we are in a culture when there are so many enquiries that there is a sense of reform fatigue. It reflects society that when there is a perception of something needing to change that a big and expensive enquiry must be set up to report on a solution that is often obvious.

The overriding objective in the civil procedure rules (the "CPR") is to resolve disputes justly and efficiently at proportionate cost and Court action is regarded as the last resort but this mantra has created a spreading species like the above mentioned Japanese Knotweed; once you have it it is difficult to get rid of. You would not want to remove all pre-action protocol, but it is long overdue for a significant pruning.

Whether the growth of pre-action protocols has led to more settlements is a matter of debate, but what is generally accepted is that it has front-loaded costs in civil litigation. Often, a client will approach their lawyer and instruct them to issue court action, but then they are confronted by what to the lay person is a prescriptive process and part of the 'tick box' trend which regulators adore. We all know the real reason behind the extensive growth in protocols; it was part of the process that began with the Woolf reforms of putting obstacles in the way of starting court action to reduce the number of cases going through the courts, because there were insufficient resources to cope. Governments did not want to invest in the civil justice system. Clients will say, "What is the point of spelling out again our case, as I have already done so to my opponent and he won't pay!". They will tell you that if there was no dispute, then I would not be instructing a lawyer. In this situation, you explain to the client that there are protocols that you are expected to comply with or else that scary monster (the cost sanction) will come knocking on your door. Faced with this, the client will usually acknowledge that you the lawyer knows best and allow you to begin the process of building up costs in complying with the protocol. But the client should beware, especially of some of the large litigation law firms who can spend an inordinate amount of money crafting an elaborate Letter of Claim.

I am not saying we should return to the old style "see you in Court in 7 days" if you do not get your cheque book out, but there certainly needs to be a re-think of pre-action protocols. I believe that the defendant should get proper notice of the intention to start Court action, but this process does not need to drag on forever and should not need you to present a thesis on the case and a mountain of accompanying documents. In some respects, I find it ironic that the parties should attempt to narrow the issues, but a detailed Letter of Claim seems to cover every alternate claim that can be imagined. To me, this displays the fact that the lawyer is unable to see the wood for the trees or is not confident to say why he believes the case will succeed. Or perhaps the lawyer is not confident enough to tell the client that some of the information he/she wants in the Letter of Claim is irrelevant. If the lawyer has carefully considered and investigated the claim, they should be able to succinctly explain the claim, attaching the key documents so that the opponent knows the case they expect to see in the court claim. A reasonable period should be given to the Defendant to consider the claim such as 28 days, but where protocols indicate a longer period, I am rather sceptical of the reason other than perhaps the opponent is an insurer and cannot pull their finger out and get around to responding sooner.

I have many years' experience of conducting Claimant debt recovery actions. In that time, I issued proceedings against individuals after having written a pre-action letter setting out the nature of the claim before commencing legal action. Experience tells me that the key to successful debt recovery was to be quick off the mark and to have a plan as to how to enforce the debt after judgment. In 2017, a new Pre-Action Protocol for Debt Claims was introduced which covered any business (including sole traders and public bodies) claiming payment of a debt from individuals (including a sole trader).

From this point in time, my desire to accept instructions to pursue a debt against an individual has declined, unless I am sure that the debtor has some obvious means of paying. In fact, I have in some respects turned from poacher to gamekeeper and get more enjoyment (and more fees) from defending money claims.

The debt action protocol is a good example of the worst in this obsession with having to comply with rules dreamt up by a committee who seem so scared of issuing a court claim. It is not good news for businesses (especially small ones) trying to get paid. It is an open invitation for consumers and sole traders to kick the issue down the road. It appears to have been created by naïve people who are too trusting. It is like the current crop of politicians who often seem to have been born into politics without first having done a job outside to gain some experience of the real world. People who have experience of business and debt recovery know that the process of recovering money needs a tight grip and people do take advantage. I am not advocating a return to a process where people sue en masse without proper attempts to negotiate or sending a proper notice before Court action, but what can happen is that a debtor can get more extensions of time than is necessary. What is often forgotten is that consumers and sole traders will get many reminders from credit control and accounts before debt claims end up going to legal action.

The debt protocol is too heavily balanced against the creditor. It was I suspect introduced (or so it is said) to avoid heavy-handed businesses and debt collectors rushing to legal action without the debtor having enough information about the debt and being given enough time to seek advice and possibly come to an arrangement. I support debtors seeking proper advice but what is objectionable is that the creditor must spend a lot more money and time sending more information to the debtor which states what in most cases they already know, and on top of that, time must be allowed to 'take stock'! A competent debt recovery person will develop a sense when a debtor is playing a game. The adage of there being those who cannot pay and those that will not pay is still generally true. There are some cases that involve possible Defences, for example over points of contractual terms, but these are in the minority. Why create a system that is not appropriate for most cases?

Every competent lawyer involved in civil litigation should take a sufficiently detailed statement from the client at the start of a matter and obtain the vital documents to enable proper advice to be given. If both sides of a potential dispute have done this then the pre-action protocol should in theory not run to more than the Letter of Claim and the Response. The Letter of Claim should set out the nature of the Claim from statements/instructions taken from the client plus the enclosures of important documents. The Defendant's lawyer (having done the same with his client) should be able to provide a response with sufficient detail so that the Claimant can appreciate the extent of the Defence. This in basic terms is the Pre-Action Practice Direction where no specific protocol applies. In my view, this should be sufficient pre-action activities to cover most areas of litigation. A more complex case may require longer to gather the response but not a great deal longer if the parties have already had discussions before instructing lawyers and will therefore understand the issues and will have the paperwork at their fingertips. However, the specific pre-action protocols are more involved than this and that is why I believe there needs to be less pre-action and more action.

Much mention is made of "proportionality" and indeed this is in the overriding objective set out in the Civil Procedure Rules, Part 1. Although proportionality applies to the extent of judicial resources allocated to a case, it also concerns the costs of litigation as a whole and therefore to pre-issue matters. The level of costs a litigant may incur will often depend on the choice of law firm. Some large city firms charge eye watering amounts for putting together a letter of claim. Their "client care letters" (terms of business letters) probably should read:

"Your matter will be handled by Fred Smith who is a qualified solicitor. However, I [Mr Big Partner] will have overall charge of your matter and I will charge extortionate rates per hour to sign letters and take credit for documents prepared by more junior lawyers in the firm. I will also be assisted by others (more junior lawyers) because there will be tasks that are beneath me or I have not got a clue how to do. If you wish to contact me, good luck, because I rarely take a call and I will get my secretary ("she who must be obeyed") to say that I am in a meeting. There will also be a charge of £50 postage for each letter (even though e-mail is sufficient, but we like to send it by e-mail, post, DX, fax and carrier pigeon just to make sure it arrives) and £10 for every staple used."

Although this is a tongue in cheek representation of a terms of engagement letter, the purpose is to highlight that there are a wide range of law firms out there and some will go overboard when it comes to charging and pre-action letters. As always though, it is horses for courses and the client has a wide choice.

Not only do you get Claimant lawyers who go overboard with pre-action protocol, but there also those Defendant lawyers who spend much of their correspondence telling you that you cannot issue proceedings because you have not complied with protocol. Even if you have not complied with the exact letter of the protocol, the relevance of pre-action conduct is to costs and the reality is that it is a high bar to impact on the general rule that costs follow the event. As well as bleating on about not being allowed to issue proceedings, they will often make a paltry offer to settle and get really annoyed if you do not reciprocate. It is as though you are not allowed to ever commence court action and must engage in endless negotiations to resolve the matter, even though your client has no intention of settling and the case is worth more than the pathetic offer they have put forward. When you look at who your opponent is on the other side in these cases, it is interesting that they are often the more recently qualified lawyers, and it is as though they are following the most recent course manual on pre-action conduct. My more cynical view is that such an approach displays a defence that is full of holes and they seek to distract from that, and they might also be one of those firms who want to cost churn. A newly qualified fee earner will be under pressure to record "chargeable time" and there is no better way to do this than to engage in repetitive pre-action correspondence.

SUMMARY

Setting out the nature of your case to your opponent before court proceedings is important but there is a tendency for pre-action protocol to be elevated to godlike status and that any deviation from it should be punishable by death. Nothing irritates me more than this slavish adherence by some lawyers to pre-action protocol. Shouts of, *"you have not provided a ten-million-page response to our latest letter so you cannot issue proceedings"* or *"you must consider making an offer"* are too often becoming the buzz phrases of young new litigators. At the end of the day, we act on instructions. Most commercial clients understand the game and want lawyers to be cunning and not to kowtow to rigid dogma. Litigation is like a game of chess, and you need to have a strategy for your client's case. You should be permitted to come up with the best strategy for your client and not have to engage in tick box exercises to satisfy the gods of protocol. Unreasonable conduct can be punished by costs decisions, but the meritless cry in pre-action correspondence that you must present your case in a certain way otherwise the world will fall apart is irritating and does not address the real legal issues in a case. Lawyers have a professional duty to preach to the client about protocol and ADR. Often this is rather insulting to the informed client who knows it is another technique to keep new claims away from Court. Perhaps if more litigants knew the other side could swiftly enforce their rights through an efficient court system, more cases would settle. The defendant without a case is often allowed to play the protocol game as they know there are

LESS PRE-ACTION, MORE ACTION

many hoops to jump through before legal action commences. There is a time for talking but there seems to be too much pre-action and not enough action.

Chapter 4

How Much to Reveal?

Disclosure aims to ensure that all the parties to a civil claim are aware of all the documents that have a bearing on the claim. The extent to which parties must provide documents to the other side which either support or undermine their case is a stage in litigation that has caused costs to grow and satellite disputes to thrive. This stage of "disclosure" has developed like a hoarder's house – clear and defined to start with but now cluttered and unnecessary.

The growth of new technology (e-mails, texts, and online apps) has greatly expanded the scope of documents to plough through and the level of costs involved. The process of disclosure can be used as a costs weapon. Opponents may deliver box loads of documents, many of which have no relevance to the issues in the case. Some might say that it was a misunderstanding of the meaning of standard disclosure, whereas others may take the view that if you present a lorry load of irrelevant documents that may either frighten the other side into making an offer because they can't be bothered to go through all the documents, or it may create the impression that the other side has a good case. There is another reason for producing a mountain of paperwork at the disclosure stage; where a party has a document in their possession which is very damaging to their case, they may want to bury it among a lot of irrelevant material in the hope that its importance goes unnoticed.

When considering how to reform disclosure, a touch of reality needs to be taken on board. The introduction of a Disclosure Pilot Scheme in January 2019 has provoked much comment. Much of the feedback from lawyers has not been favourable. A report by Professor Rachael Mulheron published in February 2020 described that of the 44 law firms consulted (mainly city law firms), 85% thought the pilot had increased costs. The article on the Law Society Gazette website which summarised this report, caused some interesting readers' comments to be left. One said:

> *"Rules committee is dominated by people who have no costs experience, no experience of dealing with clients of modest means..."*

Another comment was:

> *"So glad I'm retired. Who thinks up these stupid rules? Not someone who has ever had to deal with ordinary clients and manage their costs exposure."*

These comments and the feedback from the law firms ought to be enough to sink this ridiculous Disclosure Pilot. It seems that the Rules Committee ought to have training on common sense, and then they would realise that introducing more steps in a process causes costs to increase. Do we really need pilot schemes to prove what is blatantly obvious?

The intention of the Disclosure Pilot Scheme (DPS) was to

encourage a change in approach to disclosure in civil litigation, to "ensure disclosure is directed to the issues in the proceedings and that the scope of disclosure is not wider than is reasonable and proportionate in order to fairly resolve the issues."

Civil Procedure Rule 51U seeks to achieve this by:

1. Introducing "Initial Disclosure" of the documents relied on at the time of serving the statements of case.
2. The completion of a Disclosure Review Document before the Case Management Conference.
3. Introducing a menu of 5 models of "Extended Disclosure" involving different criteria for the extent of the search for further documents.

On the face of it, the above may seem a reasonable approach until you stop and examine what it means in practice compared to what generally takes place in cases where the DPS is not running. The Disclosure Review Document is a classic example of something which promises to improve things but all it does is to add bureaucratic layers to a process. To understand how it will add to the costs of proceedings, look at the template of the form which must be completed under the DPS.

The idea is for the parties to try to agree the issues in the case that need disclosure. In smaller cases and those which do not contain multiple parties, that could seem workable. However, where there are many parties to the litigation it has proved a "laborious" and cost increasing exercise. Whilst defining the issues for disclosure may lead to a better understanding of the case and perhaps assist in settlement,

CIVIL JUSTICE AFTER COVID

Section 1A:
Issues for Disclosure and proposed Disclosure Models

Brief description of the Issue for Disclosure[2]	Issue agreed?		Proposed Model of Extended Disclosure (A – E)		Decision (for the court)
	Reference to statement of case	Yes	No (party not agreeing)	To be completed by claimant	To be completed by defendant	
1.						
[Alternative proposed wording, if not agreed]						
2.						
3.						
4.						

[2] If the wording of any issue for Disclosure cannot be agreed, the alternative wording proposed should be included immediately under the claimants formulation.

what invariably will happen is that this will simply increase the time lawyers have to spend on the preparation for the Case Management Conference and will also increase the length of the Case Management Conference; this was identified by the research of Professor Mulheron. If the Case Management Conference is to last say 3 hours instead of 90 minutes, then the obvious implication is that will cause further delays to a case as it will take longer to find a space of 3 hours in the court list.

The process of "Initial Disclosure" which is the production of documents relied on at the time of serving the statements of case is a good move. What most objections concern is the next stage of "Extended Disclosure" and having to agree the list of issues and what model of disclosure is appropriate for each issue. Even without extended disclosure, adverse documents must be disclosed. And that is perhaps where this process should pause and a party who thinks that additional disclosure is required should simply state what it requires and why, and if it is not produced, seek a direction to that effect at the Case Management Conference.

The rule makers who think getting the parties to agree the list of issues should not be a problem if the lawyers co-operate, are naive. Whilst lawyers have an over-riding duty to the court, lawyers also have a duty to their clients and that balancing act is not always easy. A lawyer will want to be seen to be arguing for his client and not just cosily agreeing what should happen with his opposite number. It will undoubtedly be easier with some clients than others. I recall an instance during a case when I was discussing with the other side's lawyer (as requested to do so by the judge to see if the issues could be narrowed), my client becoming neurotic because he saw the two of us smiling and being pleasant towards one another. Obviously, some clients do not understand that you can assertively make your case without having to scream and shout at your opponent; or sometimes it is pointless to waste time arguing over very minor differences. However, most lawyers, because of the climate we live in with the customer always being right, will want to avoid any complaints and the hassle that they cause, and so succumb to a less co-operative attitude with the other side. The court may take a dim view of it, but it is the lesser of two evils.

There is a big assumption that having more disclosure is better than less. The disclosure pilot was an attempt to curtail the excesses of disclosure, but I would argue that it has the opposite effect. For all its criticisms as being "palm tree justice", the procedure adopted for disclosure in the small claims track is worth remembering and (with some minor adjustments) should be more widely adopted. In case you are not familiar with "palm tree justice", it is a phrase given to speedy justice applied in good faith but without paying much attention to existing law, precedent, or fundamental principles.

Below is CPR Part 27 which shows that Parts of the CPR do not apply to small claims.

Extent to which other Parts do not apply

27.2

(1) The following Parts of these Rules do not apply to small claims
   (a) Part 25 (interim remedies) except as it relates to interim injunctions;
   (b) Part 31 (disclosure and inspection);
   (c) Part 32 (evidence) except rule 32.1 (power of court to control evidence);
   (d) Part 33 (miscellaneous rules about evidence);
   (e) Part 35 (experts and assessors) except rules 35.1 (duty to restrict expert evidence), 35.3 (experts – overriding duty to the court), 35.7 (court's power to direct that evidence is to be given by single joint expert) and 35.8 (instructions to a single joint expert);
   (f) Subject to paragraph (3), Part 18 (further information);
   (g) Part 36 (offers to settle); and
   (h) Part 39 (hearings) except rule 39.2 (general rule– hearing to be in public) and rule 39.8 (communications with the court).
(2) The other Parts of these Rules apply to small claims except to the extent that a rule limits such application.

(3) The court of its own initiative may order a party to provide further information if it considers it appropriate to do so.

CPR Part 31 is the rule relating to Disclosure and cases allocated to the small claims track is not subject to the CPR Part 31, which is the rule relating to Disclosure. However, there is provision for the Court of its own initiative to order a party to provide further information if it considers it appropriate to do so.

SUMMARY

Disclosure is another area where the civil rules committee are making matters too complicated. I understand that these bodies need to have things to do but it is in keeping with the prevailing policy of making the solution worse than the problem. Open and honest disclosure depends on the integrity of those involved in litigation. Introducing more intricate models of disclosure will not overcome the situations where litigants fail to disclose adverse documents. All it does is to add time and cost to the litigation process. If a party thinks there is something missing from the opponent's disclosure, then they can always make an application to the court, hopefully before the shredding machine has been switched on.

Chapter 5

Remote Hearings. Will In-Person Hearings Become a Thing of the Past?

With the Woolf Reforms, court started to have more telephone hearings. The rules initially allowed telephones hearings if both sides were represented. Telephone hearings became popular for short hearings and where no oral evidence was to be heard such as directions hearings. Even though there was provision for telephone hearings, there were still County Courts where their lists were full of short hearings and the advocates had travelled a long way and often had to sit around for long periods waiting for their 10 min slot before the District Judge. With the outbreak of COVID, the Courts were delivered a big jolt and had to wake up to the modern world where much greater use had to be made of online technology to conduct hearings even where oral evidence was to be given. If the system did not embrace the change, and quickly, civil justice would grind to a complete standstill. Some courts did use the tactic of adjourning cases, hoping it would go away. Although we had been told that the online court was having lot of money spent of it, the actual delivery date of this online court is being pushed further down the line. With COVID, we saw the Courts and Judges grasping the importance of keeping a functioning justice system going. The key question is whether the Courts will maintain the use of video trials for civil cases after COVID?

As with anything that requires a Government department to decide, they cannot seem to do so without employing "Consultants" (and probably at great expense) to carry out politically correct research which will take several months and come to conclusions based on a small amount of data. One such report into video hearings was published in July 2020 entitled "Video Hearings Process Evaluation (Phase 2)". This was conducted by Professor Meredith Rossner and Ms Martha McCurdy of the London School of Economics. The report came up with some useful findings, but they were based on observing only 23 hearings of which 6 could not proceed because of technical problems and 3 others were adjourned to a later date so that there was time to read documents. This reminded me of a consultation that took place before a big hike in court fees, which had a small sample of contributions. Whenever Government departments undertake consultations, they have already made up their minds to do something and the exercise is one of going through the motions. Court fees is a good example of this; it did not matter if everyone who contributed to the consultation said that court fees were too high and should not go up, you can bet your life savings that court fees will increase. Court fee increases can rarely be justified and the big increase in issue fees for cases over £10,000 was simply astonishing. Having to pay a court fee of 5% of the amount over £10,000 (up to a maximum of £10,000) has certainly placed civil justice out of reach for many more people.

However, not all such reports are based on a low number of responses and one such example was, "*The impact of COVID-19 measures on the civil justice system*" which was published in June 2020. The report was prepared by Dr Natalie Byrom of the Legal Education Foundation:

The rapid review was launched on 1 May 2020 and concluded on 15 May 2020. The aim of the review was threefold:

i) *To understand the impact of the arrangements necessitated by COVID-19 on court users.*
ii) *To make practical recommendations to address any issues over the short to medium term.*
iii) *To inform thinking about a longer-term review.*

The majority of respondents to the survey were lawyers: - of the 1077 people who responded to the survey, 871 were lawyers. The survey asked respondents a number of questions about the most recent remote hearing they had participated in. Data was collected on 480 hearings in total.

A summary of its findings included:

A number of respondents made recommendations to support the continued operation of the civil justice system in the short to medium term. Suggestions included expanding the use of remote hearings in large commercial cases and maximising their use in interlocutory hearings and trials without evidence in other areas of law. Respondents emphasised the important role of continuing to list trials in encouraging parties to settle. The majority of costs disputes were also felt to be suitable for remote determination. Practical suggestions to improve the conduct of hearings included improving the equipment provided to judges and developing the functionality of platforms used to conduct remote hearings to enable better document sharing. The importance of improving systems and support for preparing and filing e-bundles and providing access to listings and case information was also referenced. In terms of policy recommendations, some respondents advocated for decisions to be taken about the types of legal problems that should be dealt with by the civil justice system respondents recommended considering whether claims brought in relation to private parking could be dealt with via different arrangements.

The spread of COVID in March 2020 forced the Civil Courts to take urgent measures to keep the legal process functioning, albeit in ways not widely used before. The introduction of more Hearings by video (on platforms such as Skype, Zoom or Teams) enabled some Trials to take place. The obvious question is after COVID, should the Courts return to having Trials in person?

It is often argued that remote Hearings make it difficult for the Judge to assess the credibility of a witness. This places importance on the demeanor of a witness. In simple terms, does the way the witness presents his evidence and how they look impact on whether the evidence is believed? Is it easier for a Judge to decide if the witness is telling the truth if they are not physically present in Court? I would say that demeanor is important in some types of hearings, for example in Criminal Proceedings and Family cases, but it is not a great basis for assessing credibility in civil cases. The point, that placing too much weight on demeanor is irrational, was well put by Leggatt L J in **R(SS) in Secretary of State for Home Department** when it was said:

"Rather than attempting to assess whether testimony is truthful from the manner in which it is given, the only objective and reliable approach is to focus on the content of the testimony and to consider whether it is consistent with other evidence (including evidence of what the witness has said on other occasions) and with known or probable facts."

This has surely got to be the appropriate way to assess credibility. Focusing solely on the demeanor of the witness could lead to the danger of irrational decisions because a Judge takes a dislike to a person's attitude and appearance. It works both ways in that a Judge may wrongly think that a well-dressed, well-spoken, and well-educated person is telling the truth in the same way as a scruffy and poor mannered person may be regarded as discreditable.

The key to assessing the credibility of evidence is to look for inconsistencies. A good advocate will tell you that this is the secret of good cross examination. You should look at what has previously been written down and in Witness Statements exchanged in evidence and try to highlight inconsistencies. During cross examination, you question the witness about these apparent inconsistencies and hope that the witness will not have convincing answers or says something different which causes confusion or comes down firmly on your side. If the previous documentation and the prepared Witness Statement shows no inconsistencies, it makes cross examination much more difficult. If the witness sticks firmly to what is stated in his/her statement and other documentation, that leaves the advocate with little to challenge the witness on as he cannot keep asking the same questions if the answer is clear but is not what was wanted. There may be a small element of considering whether a witness looks uncomfortable when giving their answers, but this could be explained by other factors such as nervousness or culture. In some cultures, it is not normal practice to look another straight in the eye when talking.

Considering the above, assessing the credibility of witnesses is not as greatly affected by having a remote Hearing. What is more affected by remote Hearings is the flow of proceedings as cross examination is more difficult because of the time lags that often exist due to the different speeds of internet connections. The technological delay makes it difficult to know when someone has stopped speaking and causes participants to talk over others. These problems can probably be overcome with improved platforms and faster connections. Also, signals can be introduced to know when it is time to speak and time to stop. This may not overcome some of the problems for the advocates who often sense whether their questions or submissions are having an impact on the Judge by keeping an eye on their reactions. In remote Hearings, the camera may not always be on the Judge when the advocate is speaking.

Being able to quickly glance around the Court and assess the reaction of the Judge is important to how an advocate pitches their submissions. I recall from my early occasions before a District Judge in Chambers that it is important to keep an eye on the Judge and not simply plough on regardless. You might need to vary the speed of delivery to allow the Judge to take a note; other times you can gauge that the Judge is looking disinterested in what you are saying and so it is time to move on to another submission. Sometimes a Judge will interrupt an advocate and pose a question; whilst you might attempt to respond with a convincing answer, if you cannot think of a good instant answer, acknowledge the point and move onto another submission. If you do not you risk not having time to make a better point on which the Judge may be with you.

There are greater issues than assessing demeanour and technological glitches. The place where a witness gives evidence is an important consideration. A witness needs to be in a quiet room with no other person around who can feed them the answer to difficult questions. Ideally, this would be in the offices of their legal representative but that may involve travel, or the party may be a litigant in person. Giving evidence in the comfort of your own home may be less stressful but do the Proceedings have the same formality and seriousness if you are at the kitchen table in your pajama bottoms? Will the Court process be given the respect if you are not present in a Court building? I do not believe this is a big issue when you see how some people already behave in a Courtroom. It is far more important that the civil justice system provides a method whereby it is easier to attend and give evidence. Many people are discouraged from giving evidence because of the stress of the experience but also because of the sheer inconvenience. With the centralisation of Courts following the large closure program, the commute is sometimes a difficulty and getting time off work may not be easy or involves unpaid leave. The travel and the hanging around waiting for Hearings to start, means a whole day is given up. Having the Hearing remotely could mean the witness going into a room at work to give evidence and then can get back to their job without the time and cost involved in traveling back from the Court building. It could lead to an improvement in justice as cases will have more witnesses to give the relevant evidence and increase the prospects of the right outcome. Unavailable witnesses mean adjournments or witnesses being summoned against their will and a reluctant witness is not always a good witness.

One area of remote Hearings which could be disadvantageous to parties is the ease by which they can consult with their lawyers during the Hearing. Where the Hearing takes place in person it is easy for the lawyer to pause for a moment and take instructions from the client or for notes to be passed under the advocate's nose. However, is this process really compromised by remote Hearings? During a remote, it is quite easy for the client and their lawyers to email messages to their advocate during the Trial. I know advocates who have two computer screens in front of them so that it is easier to monitor messages that are coming in real-time. The danger of receiving messages in real time (by emails and online messages) is that this could be used to prompt witnesses to give the answers a party wants to hear rather than the truth.

It is fair to say that there is no reason why most Court Hearings, except where there are many witnesses or where the documentation is vast, should not be conducted by video link over the internet. The cost savings are substantial to the parties in that their lawyers are not having to charge for travel time and the lawyers can more easily do other work while waiting for a remote Hearing to start. If a lawyer is stuck in the waiting room at some dingy inner city County Court, doing other work on other cases it is not easy; there are confidentiality issues with discussing sensitive matters in a public place and old Court buildings seem to have a poor Wi-Fi signal. Being in the office (or working from home) while waiting for a Trial to start enables the lawyer to keep an eye on other matters. If the worst happens and the Hearing is adjourned, then time is not wasted trudging back to the office on a crowded train or crawling through the traffic jams.

Some may say that lawyers do conduct conversations about cases in places they should not. Contrary to popular belief, junior barristers and lawyers travel in the crowded standard class on trains. I am amazed by the way some lawyers discuss their client's business in full earshot of other commuters on the morning train. You never know if your opposing lawyer is sitting in the same carriage. When you hand your Skeleton Argument to the other advocate at the Court building and he says, *'I already know this from your conversation this morning on the 7.20 from Guildford,'* you know you have been rumbled. I am not saying that it is ever right to discuss cases in public areas, but it is difficult for barristers and other Court lawyers to avoid having to do work on the train or in other inappropriate places. I am aware of a barrister who conducted a short Hearing while riding a motorbike down the motorway with the phone headset inside their helmet.

Whether remote hearing will become the norm will depend to a large degree on whether the parties and the lawyers are satisfied with the experience. Early indications from reports for the Civil Justice Council suggest that the reaction to remote hearings is generally positive. It would seem though that there is a difference in satisfaction depending on the level of court. The higher the level of court the greater the level of satisfaction with the remote hearing process. There are though, some concerns expressed by lawyers that remote hearings do not work so well where litigants in person are involved.

SUMMARY

COVID certainly brought forward the greater use of remote hearings. It demonstrated that not enough use of remote hearings was being made by the court system. Not every case is suited to a full remote hearing such as where there are several important witnesses and the careful cross-examination of them is the key to establishing their credibility. Demeanour is not the only way of assessing credibility but what is certainly true is that cross-examination remotely does not have the same flow as when it is done in person. During COVID, having remote hearings usually meant the advocates and their clients being in separate places and most likely at home. With COVID restrictions being lifted, if parties can travel to their lawyers' offices, it would seem sensible that they might as well travel to court. Having the client present with you during a hearing is preferable as advocates can easily take instructions as matters arise. One would hope though that remote hearings will be utilised in more interim hearings and smaller matters as the savings in time and costs are so obvious that is common sense to continue their use.

REMOTE HEARINGS

Chapter 6

Changes to the Court Rules and Processes

In previous chapters there has been discussion about cost budgeting and disclosure but primarily there needs to be reform to the current structure of small claims, fast track and multitrack. The purpose would be to achieve a judicial decision as quickly as possible with the appropriate amount of costs and time being spent on the case. Litigants want their case to be determined quickly, fairly and at reasonable cost. Then, once they have a judgment, they expect to be able to recover their money and costs; for that, an efficient system is needed.

The 'lower end' of the civil courts (and perhaps the neglected part of the courts) is the County Court. I say neglected because the High Court has had considerable resources pumped into it (especially the Chancery Division) in the shape of the shiny new and modern Rolls Building on Fetter Lane. But many cases do not reach the dizzy heights of the High Court and must make do with the 'standard class' of the County Court. As with all things, there are good aspects, but many features cause extreme irritation. There is a limit as to what can be done to provide a more efficient decision-making body. If you ask the average litigant at the lower end of the civil courts, they will choose speed and efficiency over complex and lengthy procedures.

Outside the small claims track, there is a tendency to get bogged down in case management and the strict adherence to rules of procedure and evidence. In multitrack cases, much court time is wasted with Costs and Case Management Conferences. Although, parties can and should try to agree directions, such agreements happen close to a CCMC and so the time in the court list cannot be used for other cases.

Litigants want a quick decision in their dispute. Generally, this happens in small claims cases, except in some County Courts where there is a long wait for a Hearing. There is much to praise the small claims track for resolving disputes. The Court is supposed to be investing large sums in the so called 'online court', but there are concerns that it will not have enough 'proper judge' involvement. Also, there is a concern that commencing a claim will be like completing an online application for insurance rather than setting out your claim in the traditional way. Rather than commit to such a large spend on a project, why not build upon a small claims style Hearing and procedure for claims up to £25,000.

Online filing

A Claim Form and supporting documents should all be uploaded to a cloud-based platform. The Defence and supporting documents should also be uploaded. I cannot understand why a simple online 'E' filing system has not yet been developed for the County Court. People may wonder, have I forgotten Money Claims Online? I mean online filing where each document can be simply uploaded to an allocated folder. I am no IT expert, but it would be relatively straightforward to set up such an 'E' filing system.

New Rules for Service of Claims

The Civil Procedure Rules in 1998 abolished the ancient rule that proper service of proceedings meant what it said - that a defendant should receive a claim form, but the dramatic change was not quickly apparent.

There can be good service on a defendant's last known residence or last known place of business [CPR Part 6.9], even though the defendant has not actually received the document. In *Akram v Adam* **[2004] EWCA Civ 1601**, this was found to be compliant with article 6 of the European Convention on Human Rights, provided there was an opportunity for the defendant to come to the court subsequently.

There were subsequent changes to the rule so that CPR Part 6.9(3) now in summary says:

- A claimant must take "reasonable steps" to ascertain the current address.
- If the current address is found, then service must take place at that address.
- If the current address cannot be found the claimant must consider whether there is an alternative place or method of service.
- If there is an alternative place or method the claimant

must make an application under rule 6.15 (service by an alternative method or an alternative place).
- It is only when an alternative place or alternative method cannot be ascertained that the claimant can safely (or reasonably safely) serve at the last known address.

So, it is still possible for a Claim to be deemed served when the Defendant has not received it. For the legal system of England and Wales, one consequence has been a great deal of wasteful satellite litigation to establish the current law and it caused substantial unfairness in view of the burden put onto a defendant in a CPR Part 13.3 application. **CPR 13.3 (1)** permits the court to set aside a default judgment on two grounds:

- that the Defendant has a real prospect of successfully defending the claim,
- that there is some other reason why the judgment should be set aside or varied, or the defendant should be allowed to defend the claim.

The addition of the need to take *"reasonable steps"* to ascertain the current address is an open invitation to satellite litigation on what it means. However, my biggest objection to Claims being deemed served is that the above exercise of reasonable steps is open to abuse by less scrupulous creditors. The justification for a system where service can be deemed to have happened even though the Claim Form has not been received is that there are slippery debtors who want to avoid service. That is undoubtedly true in some cases but I disapprove of the consequence for another reason, which Lord Denning neatly described as a *'fundamental principle of our law'*, that *'no one is to be found guilty or made liable by an order of any tribunal unless he has been given fair notice of the proceedings so as to enable him to appear and defend them'*

In North America, it is normal for process serving to be mandatory and undertaken only by professionals or at least for claims to be evidenced by receipted post. It is obvious that to have a rule which requires a Claim to be personally served or sent by recorded delivery will increase costs but on balance I believe this is necessary to avoid unscrupulous creditors obtaining default judgment knowing full well that the debtor was not at the address to which the Claim was sent. It is not unheard of that some slippery debt collectors will use the tactic of sending to an address (or putting an address on the Claim Form for the Court to send) where the defendant is no longer in residence. In these cases, where the merits of the claim may be less than good and by getting a default judgment and then moving quickly to enforcement puts them in a position of power. Some people, faced with a bailiff at their house about to take away their car, can be in a vulnerable position and unfairly backed into a corner. I have indeed acted for clients in this position, who have had to pay something on the doorstep and then it took many months and additional costs to get the judgment set aside. Having a rule which requires the claimant to prove the claim came to the notice of the defendant would also reduce the amount of court time wasted by applications to set aside judgment. This would surely be a better use of resources.

In summary, I would want the rule on service of Claims to be amended so that a defendant must receive the Claim

Form, and this should be done by way of personal service. It may appear an extreme measure, but this could be made more palatable by allowing reasonable fixed costs to be added to be recovered for process server fees even in small claims. It will make creditors and debt collection companies unhappy, but it may also make them think carefully about those people who are worth suing rather than pursuing the sausage factory mentality of issuing thousands of claims. If this produces more work for process servers, then in theory this should lead to competition and economies of scale where larger process serving firms could offer lower rates. Alternatively, large law firms could employ their own in-house process servers to serve Claims.

Extended Court Hours

A judge's day is not simply sitting in Court from 10am to 4pm It also carries a large burden of 'box' work (paperwork) on current and future cases. One understands that Judges will have subsequent Judgments to write outside of the courtroom and that will take up their time. As to box work, there is a need to have more judicial appointments to deal with paperwork.

There had been experiments with longer and more flexible court room hours before the COVID crisis. Pilot schemes were launched in Brentford County Court and Manchester Civil Justice Centre in September 2019. These pilots were modest in their extent. In Brentford, the additional hours included an extra court session one day a week from 8am to 10.30 am and an extra court session one day a week from 4.30pm to 7pm. In Manchester, the pilot consisted of an extra two courts which would sit an extra session on Monday and Wednesday from 4.30pm to 7pm.

The pilot appears a perfectly sensible way to adjust court hours to suit the court user. After all, the Civil Courts provide a service and therefore one would expect them to try to accommodate the court user. Having more flexible court hearing times would suit parties and witnesses who find it difficult to take time off work during the day. The reaction from the Law Society and the Bar Counsel to longer court hours was not that encouraging. They warned of the difficulties it may create for some practitioners and that it would discriminate against others who, for example would find managing a family life difficult. An article for "Counsel Magazine" in November 2017 by Morwenna Macro set out some of the practical difficulties:

"Practical obstacles
The practical obstacles thrown up by early and late shifts include the following:

- *No time for case preparation.*
- *No time to meet clients before and after court.*

Arriving for 7am becomes impossible. Few barristers are confined to working in a local court and many regularly travel three hours plus to court. We cannot forgo a proper night's sleep and be productive. Public transport does not cater well for early travel.
Childcare is rarely available before 7am and after 7pm (and even those hours are hard to cover). This includes nannies, who not only deserve their own home life, but are covered by working time regulations.
   The early and late shifts of course will also negatively impact

upon many court users (parties, witnesses, victims, jurors, those that attend regularly as part of their job such as housing officers, social workers, expert witnesses) with children and who must also travel to court, which is not always close to home. The shift system may also in reality erode the current flexibility of the court day to accommodate urgent or over-running cases, and the shorter shifts will make cases last longer."

Some of the objections relate to the added pressure put on barrister's who would have less time after court in the evenings to prepare for their case the next day. This is understandable criticism of longer court hours, but the reality is if there were longer court hours then barrister's and other lawyers would have more opportunities and it would not necessarily mean they would have to spend longer in court. I believe it would be a positive thing for barrister's and other lawyers because there is an excess number of barristers chasing too few cases. Whilst I have sympathy for lawyers trying to balance home life with work, the legal profession involves a vast range of work and not all of it includes court work. There is, in my opinion, too much of an expectation that employers and work environments should be driven by the requirements of those who work in it rather than it be adapted to meet its customers. Whilst measures can be taken to assist workers from a range of home circumstances, at the end of the day if the court users find it hard to access justice, they will not want to use the civil justice system and there will be fewer places for lawyers to work in. Also, some court staff and those who run the Civil Justice system, seem to have forgotten that their purpose is to serve court users. If the system expects litigants to pay ever increasing court fees, then it is reasonable to expect a proper level of service. In most sectors of society, if you are dissatisfied with the level of service, you will use another business. The phrase "business" may raise a few eyebrows, but successive Governments have shifted it this way by expecting civil courts to be largely self-funding through courts fees.

It is important that lawyers should have the ability to work flexibly but I do not believe that the Civil Justice system should be built around the preferences of its lawyers. The Civil Justice system should serve all who use it. If there are long sitting hours, perhaps split into three sessions in the day, e.g. morning, afternoon and evening sessions, then there is the opportunity for lawyers to take on cases at a time of day which suits them.

Unless the profession is prepared to agree to longer and more flexible working hours, then the Courts will find other ways to overcome the backlog and delays in the system. These alternatives will not be so favourable to the court user such as increasing court fees or pushing more people into other forms of dispute resolution. This would go against the principle of the ordinary person having better access to civil justice.

Undoubtedly there will be some negative impact on the profession but to simply say that there should be more efficient use of existing courts and more courts available is not the whole solution. The problem with Court hours is that, as I have said in other parts of this book, too much Court time is wasted with case management hearings and cost budgeting. The judicial day in a typical County Court starts at 10am and sits through until 4pm. When you take out a lunch break that leaves only 5 hours of court room time. I do not believe it is unreasonable to expect Court to sit a little longer starting at 9.30am and going through until 5.30pm. Many people would regard these as normal working hours and probably wonder why Courts should not sit for an hour longer each day if it allows more cases to be heard. There is also a good argument for having evening court sittings to allow for parties and witnesses who find it difficult to attend normal court hours because of work. Having additional sittings on certain evenings from 6pm to 9pm would also improve the throughput of court cases.

Although more courts and longer hours are being utilised to get through a backlog of cases due to COVID, the question is will this continue when the country gets back to normal life. The limiting factor will obviously be the cost, which has always been at the heart of why the civil justice system has been crumbling over recent years. If courts make proper use of new technology and continue to use video hearings for as many hearings as possible, then the costs of extending court hours should not be so prohibitive. Many of the small claims could be dealt with in the evening court sessions by video hearings, and remote hearings are cheaper to operate without all the costs of having a building open at night for face to face hearings. If more court hearings can be catered for, then in the long run, more income will be generated, because there will more court hearing fees being charged.

A New Small Claims Track
A claim up to £25,000 should be started in the same way a claim commences now, by the issuing of a Claim Form (N1). In the small claims track, I would leave the court to serve it

as they do now, unless the Claimant has a lawyer acting for them. If a Defence is filed, then the Court should allocate the case to a District Judge to hear the case remotely by video conference without the need to send out the pointless Directions Questionnaire. In small claims, I believe the sending out of the Direction Questionnaire is a waste of time and admin costs.

If these small claims were heard remotely by video conference, that would mean fewer court rooms. The money saved and the reduced admin could be used to recruit more Deputy District Judges. Deputy District Judges are currently required to sit 20 days per year and get paid a low daily rate of about £500. These Deputy District Judges should be encouraged to hold these remote Hearings at more flexible times such as in the evenings and weekends. If the Hearing fees (or a part of it) were actually paid to the Judges, then there may be an incentive for them to hear more cases and to sit longer hours, thus increasing the number of cases that get heard. It does not take a genius to work out that if they heard, say, 4 small claims in a day at a Hearing fee of £455 each (the current Hearing fee for claims from £5000 to £10,000), the Deputy District Judge would earn more than their current day rate.

There are many exceptionally good Deputy District Judges, but I have come across some who create the impression that they are trying to move cases off their desk and with little enthusiasm to hear cases. I recall a small claim where both parties had traveled a long way for the small claim of about £5,000 to be heard. The Court had allocated 2 hours for the trial and when we went in before the Judge, after spending 10 minutes reading the file, she decided that the case was not going to be completed in the time estimate. She made it clear that she was not going to sit a minute past 4pm. Both parties were disappointed with the attitude of the Judge, but despite the objections, she adjourned it and the case was transferred to a different court. The claim was eventually heard some 3 months later, and the Hearing was completed within 45 minutes.

There are other ways a small claims procedure needs to be tweaked. Fixed legal fees should be recoverable. This would encourage the parties (especially the Claimant) to obtain some basic legal advice at the start of the matter. It would lead to litigants setting out more clearly their Particulars of Claim and Defence; this would make it easier for the Judge to understand the claim from the papers before the matter is heard.

Without clear Statements of Case, cases get delayed with directions to produce additional information to clarify matters. If the small claims track were to be increased to cases up to £25,000, then there could be sliding scale of fixed recoverable legal fees to the winner such as: -

Up to £5,000	£300
Above £5,000 but not exceeding £15,000	£800
Above £15,000 to £25,000	£1,200

Most small claims can be tried within a time estimate of 2 hours. As the small claims level would have increased to £25,000 under this proposal, there would perhaps be a need to have slightly longer to hear cases, but most should be completed within 3 hours, especially if the number of witnesses were limited to 2 on each side.

CHANGES TO THE COURT RULES AND PROCESSES

If upon the Court referring a claim of up to £25,000 in value to a Deputy District Judge, it appeared more complex and involved difficult points of law, it would be for the Judge to allocate it to a different track. The revised small claims track should be given a new name of 'the fast-track'. Cutting out the procedure of the Court sending out a Directions Questionnaire and allowing the Judge to send out a Trial date direct to the parties will speed up the process and justify the name of 'fast track'. I have always wondered why the current fast-track is so named; the reality is that a fast-track case of between £15,000 and £25,000 can take 12 months to come to Trial. My new styled 'fast- track' process should be able to deliver a Hearing date within 90 days. In times of high demand, I envisage a process whereby the County Courts, using appropriate lawyers, such as barristers of an appropriate level of experience, being authorised by the Court to decide small claims. In this respect, the process is drawing on a form of arbitration expert determination. The Court would make the selection rather than in arbitration where the parties try to agree the arbitrator. The Court could have an approved panel of lawyers it could call on to hear small claims.

At least by having a Court panel of appointed/registered barristers to conduct small claims, the panel can be reasonably satisfied that there is not going to be pressure from either party to accept a particular arbitrator. This panel of barristers whom the courts could call upon to try this new fast track small claims process would be of at least 5 years' experience. It would be open to solicitors and legal executives to be on this register of Deputy District Judges who perhaps could be given the title of Reserve Judges, as they would be called into action at times of high demand.

This amended small claims track would retain the current procedure of each party exchanging copies of the documents they wish to rely on at the Hearing. However, I would make it a requirement that the Claimant must produce any documents it relies on with the Claim Form when the claim is issued. Likewise, the Defendant should also be required to produce documents on which it wants to rely at the time of filing the Defence. Any Witness Statements of oral evidence would be required to be exchanged 14 days before the Hearing date as usually happens in small claims. If the Defence is required to file documents it relies on with the Defence, then it is reasonable to provide for a longer period in which to file the Defence. I would provide for 5 weeks (35 days) from the date of service of the Claim Form in which to file and exchange the Defence, along with documents relied upon. I would remove the 'Acknowledgement of Service' from the process as this appears unnecessary.

The date of service of claim forms would be as follows:

1. If served in person – the day the Claim is served if served before 5pm
2. If delivered to the address of the Defendant – the next working day after it was hand delivered.
3. If sent by first class post, the 3rd day after it was posted, (unless that day is Sunday or Bank Holiday, in which case it would be the following day.

I would make it a requirement of the rules before allowing a claim to be issued that the Claimant be required to provide evidence of sending a Notice of Claim in writing to the

CHANGES TO THE COURT RULES AND PROCESSES

Defendant which gives the Defendant 28 days to respond in a straightforward debt claim. If the Claimant is not able to produce evidence of this 28-day letter, then the Claimant would not be permitted to issue the claim.

With the period for responding to a claim increased from 28 days to 35 days, the rules about permitting an extension of time would operate on the presumption that an extension would not be granted unless a good reason is provided. Currently, the parties can agree an extension of up to 28 days, but I would reduce that to 21 days bearing in mind that under my proposal of there being 35 days from the date of service to file Defence, the Defendant has already been given an extra week. If a defendant requires more time to file a Defence then it must make an application to the court to show a good reason why it needs an extension of time.

Once a Defence is entered the Court would be required to locate/allocate it to a DJ/DDJ or Reserve Judge within a set period (2 weeks) and the Judge who receives the allocation is required to notify the parties of their appointment within 14 days asking the parties to notify the Judge within 7 days of dates to avoid for the Hearing within the next 3 months. The Judge then sets a date for the small claims Hearing with 21 days' notice.

So, the timeline for this new 'small claim track' would be as follows: -

1. Claimant sends a Claim Form, and the documents relied on, to County Court and requests that a claim be issued. The Claim Form would be slightly different to the current form N1.
2. Court gives the claim a number and returns a sealed copy

to the Clainant to serve on the Defendant if the Claimant has legal representation.
3. The Defendant would have 35 days from the date of service to file and serve the Defence along with documents relied upon.
4. The Court within 2 weeks of receiving the Defence, allocates it to a Judge for a remote Hearing.
5. The Judge notifies the parties of his appointment within 2 weeks and the parties give dates to avoid within 7 days.
6. The Judge notifies the parties of a Hearing date which should be within 3 months of the Defence.
7. The parties to file and serve any Witness Statements 14 days before the Hearing.

The new "middle-track" (new suggested name for fast-track cases)

At present the fast-track covers claims that exceed £10,000 but do not exceed £25,000. I would propose this track be renamed "middle-track" to remove the misleading name of "fast track" when the track is not always particularly fast. This new middle-track would cover claims that exceed £25,000 but do not exceed £100,000. This would be a big extension of the current fast-track but there is a good argument to extend its range. One of the justifications is there are many claims that are in the multi-track value bracket but do not need the same treatment in terms of directions as the Multi-Track. Yes, there is provision for the parties to agree the fast track instead of the multi-track, but even where parties agree there are situations where the court will spend time considering if it is appropriate. One of the main factors in considering if

CHANGES TO THE COURT RULES AND PROCESSES

a case will currently be in the fast track is whether the trial will take longer than a day. In court time that translates to 5 hours. Many cases at the lower end of the Multi-Track might take a little longer than a day but do not warrant being in the multi-track.

The current standard directions for a fast-track matter are as follows: (CPR Practice Direction 28.3.12. The table set out below contains a typical timetable the court may give for the preparation of the case.)

Disclosure	4 *weeks*
Exchange of witness statements	10 *weeks*
Exchange of experts' reports	14 *weeks*
Sending of pre-trial check lists (listing questionnaires) by the court	20 *weeks*
Filing of completed pre-trial check lists	22 *weeks*
Hearing	30 *weeks*

These periods will run from the date of the notice of allocation.

There will of course be more detailed directions in some instances but the above represents the basic core directions of a fast-track matter. Cases in the fast-track tend to take longer than the expected 30 weeks to reach trial.

My new suggested "middle-track" would have various changes in addition to the fact it would cover claims above £25,000 to £100,000:

- A middle-track claim would be where a trial would take up to 2 days.
- There would generally be a limit of 2 witnesses per party.

- Expert evidence would generally be by way of written reports.
- Fixed legal costs (excluding court fees):
- Maximum of £20,000 for cases above £25,000 to £60,000
- Maximum of £40,000 for cases from £60,000 to £100,000
- Where it is a non-monetary claim: maximum of £35,000.

The figure for fixed legal costs is admittedly rather arbitrary at this stage, but the general principle that the level of fixed costs should be that there is a sliding scale based on the amount of the claim, the number of days at trial and the complexity of the case.

A new "upper-track"

At present, the multi-track covers cases that have a value of over £25,000. This generally covers the more complex cases. I would replace the multi-track with a new "upper-track" that covers case with a value of over £100,000 and where the trial is likely to last more than 2 days.

The stages in this new upper limit would in many ways match those of the current multi-track. However, removing costs budgeting would reduce the amount of time taken at the Case Management Conference. I would again set fixed costs for cases in the upper-track. Again, this in the early stages would be a rather arbitrary calculation but I would suspect a sliding structure such as the following:

- Cases above £100,000 up to £600,000 – a maximum of £300,000.
- Cases over £600,000 up to £3 million – a maximum of £500,000
- Cases over £3 million – a maximum of £2 million

CHANGES TO THE COURT RULES AND PROCESSES

Lawyers would be allowed to agree with their clients that the client can be requested to pay their legal fees which exceed the fixed levels. It means that the client will know that if they win the case, the maximum they will be entitled to recover is the fixed amount from the other side. If there are fixed legal fees than clients will most likely put pressure on lawyers to agree a fee that does not exceed the fixed levels. That in time will have the effect of reducing legal fees and perhaps will mean that litigation might become slightly more accessible. It might even make obtaining legal insurance a little easier as the underwriters will know how much they are potentially having to cover.

Now in some circles, there will be resistance to fixed legal costs. This perhaps could be tempered by giving the court the discretion to allow indemnity costs if there has been misconduct by the losing party in the litigation. This potential threat of indemnity costs for unreasonable conduct might be an incentive that creates better case management and compliance with directions.

At the end of a trial, it does not automatically mean that the winning party would be awarded the fixed level of costs. That could in some situations lead to costs being disproportionate. For example, if the case was valued at £150,000 and the winning lawyers spent say £200,000, then although the maximum fixed cost in this bracket would be £300,000, the judge would be asked to consider if the sum claimed was proportionate.

The typical sequence of steps in an upper track case would be:

1. Case issued.
2. Defendant has 35 days from the date of service to file a Defence. The parties can agree an extension of up to 21 days. Beyond that, court permission is required.
3. Directions
4. Standard Disclosure
5. Witness Statements
6. Expert evidence (if necessary)
7. Trial

Rather than having a Case Management Hearing listed upon the return of the Directions Questionnaire, I would have a prescribed list of directions which apply in most cases and the parties can agree to extend these dates by up to 21 days. Beyond that, they would need permission of the Court.

Example:
Big Commercial Company Ltd v. Brian Slime
Big Commercial Company Ltd ("BCCL") contracted with Hacked Computers Ltd ("HC") to install a new accounting system on their computers at a price of £120,000. The new software system according to BCCL does not function as it was represented to them by HC. HC argue that the software is compatible with the computers BCCL told them they had and so it is not a fault with the software. BCCL instructed lawyers to write a letter before action and HC lawyers responded denying liability. BCCL issues proceedings and HC has 35 days from the deemed date of service to file a Defence. HC asks BCCL for additional time to file a Defence. BCCL agrees an extra 14 days. Upon the filing of the Defence, the Court would send out a Notice of Allocation to the Upper-Track

CHANGES TO THE COURT RULES AND PROCESSES

and with that Notice a List of Directions. The directions might comprise the following:

1. Standard Disclosure by List within 8 weeks of the Notice and inspection 14 days thereafter.
2. Witness statements to be exchanged 6 weeks after Inspection.
3. Expert reports (if required) to be filed 6 weeks after witness statements.
4. The parties receive a trial date after the exchange of witness statements (or after the filing of expert evidence if required), by completing a trial questionnaire.

The purpose behind this rather streamlined approach to directions is that there is an absence of case management. The usual position would be a Case Management Conference, but not having one would free up more time in the court list for the hearing of trials. As I have discussed earlier, "Costs and Case Management Conferences" which can be listed for 1.5 to 2 hours is a poor use of court time. As I have argued for the abolition of costs budgeting, that would remove the main reason for Case Management Conferences.

SUMMARY

The suggestions in this chapter are designed to make litigation more straightforward and as a result less expensive. In addition, cases should arrive at a judicial decision more quickly. There needs to be a concerted effort by officials in the Ministry of Justice and elsewhere to move away from designing complicated solutions to issues which often seem like a deliberate attempt to put obstacles in the way of using the court process. What most litigants want is a procedure that is fair but will deliver a decision within a reasonable period and at a reasonable cost. What they do not want is a system that gets sidetracked on satellite litigation and convoluted arguments over procedures.

Chapter 7

Relief from Relief?

The courts obsession with procedural default is unjust. Cases should not be decided by minor breaches of procedure but on the substantive issues. When the County Court loses the court file or fails to give the trial judge the skeleton arguments of the parties, no sanctions are applied, nor compensation provided. Before the introduction of the Civil Procedure Rules (CPR) in April 1999, the courts took a justice-based approach to procedural default. The introduction of the CPR in 1999 did not significantly change the approach. From April 2013, the position became draconian. This new style of over- reaction to a breach of rules is rather like the chefs over-reaction in the Monty Python "Restaurant Sketch" to a complaint about a dirty fork. Like the dirty fork, the breach of the rules can and should in my view be dealt with in a better and more proportionate way; whereas the Courts prefer to take the approach of that John Cleese character and erupt with rage and slam a large knife into the table.

From 1 April 2013, CPR 3.9 was amended to provide that on an application for relief from any sanction imposed for a failure to comply with any rule, practice direction or court order:

"the court will consider all the circumstances of the case, so as to enable it to deal justly with the application, including the need –

(a) for litigation to be conducted efficiently and at proportionate cost; and
(b) to enforce compliance with rules, practice directions and orders".

These two factors replaced the previous (non-exhaustive) list of nine circumstances the court would consider on such applications, which included whether the application for relief had been made promptly, whether the failure to comply was intentional, whether there was a good explanation for it, and the effect of both the failure and the grant of relief on each party. The amended rule applies to applications made on or after 1 April 2013.

From that date, there was also an amendment to the "overriding objective", to which the court must seek to give effect whenever it exercises any powers, or interprets any rule, under the Civil Procedure Rules (CPR). The amendment made it clear that dealing with cases justly and at proportionate cost includes "enforcing compliance with rules, practice directions and orders".

The amendments sought to implement Lord Justice Jackson's recommendation that the courts *"should be less tolerant than hitherto of unjustified delays and breaches of orders"*. The purpose behind the amendments was to force a change of culture, whereby breaches of court orders would not be tolerated as readily as they were previously, as well as to simplify the rule. These amendments brought about a significant change in culture, in that the courts are more likely to make tough case management decisions where parties are in breach of rules or court orders and less willing to grant relief from sanctions in the event of a breach. The courts are also stricter in granting extensions of time for compliance with rules and orders.

In **Denton v TH White Ltd [2014] EWCA Civ 906**, the Court of Appeal set out a three-stage approach to be applied in applications for relief from sanctions under CPR r. 3.9:

Stage 1: Was the breach that gave rise to the sanction "serious or significant".

Stage 2: Do the reason(s) for the breach suggest that the sanction ought not to be applied.

Stage 3: The court must then consider all the circumstances of the case to deal with the application for relief "justly". The rule specifies two factors: the need for litigation to be conducted efficiently and at proportionate cost, along with the need to enforce compliance with rules, practice directions and orders.

A few first instance decisions after the reforms were implemented highlighted a tension between the increased focus on compliance and the desire to do justice in the individual case. The Court of Appeal's decision in **Andrew Mitchell MP v News Group Newspapers Limited [2013] EWCA Civ 1537** came down firmly on the side of compliance but that approach was tempered by the subsequent decision in **Denton v TH White Ltd, Decadent Vapours Ltd v Bevan, Utilise TDS Ltd v Davies [2014] EWCA Civ 906.**

The idea behind the change in April 2013 was totally misguided. It stems from the belief that all hold-ups in the civil justice system are derived from a culture of non-compliance. This ignores the key part played by a lack of capacity and resources. Previous sections of this book have highlighted how the number of people working in the Court Service has declined along with a decline in the number of judges. I wish those responsible for bringing forward such changes as that which happened to CPR 3.9 in 2013 would be honest about its motives. It followed a mass closure of courts in 2012 and with the number of cases being issued not falling, there was always going to be this tightening up of compliance with court rules as a mechanism for the early disposal of cases. It is a very short-sighted approach and leads to injustice as genuine cases are disposed of for breaches of procedure rather than on the substantive law or the facts in issues. A clever but unfair process for adjusting demand with the available supply. In the long run, the architect of this blunt instrument had not given sufficient thought to the spin off satellite litigation which has arguably eaten up more court resources than the original alleged problem. I deliberately use the words "alleged original problem" because I am not convinced that since the changes introduced by Woolf that there has been a culture of delay and non-compliance.

The problem with relief from sanctions is that the civil justice process has become cluttered with cases that any common-sense approach would apply the principle of "de minimis non curat lex" (the law is not concerned with trivial things). The Court of Appeal said in Mitchell:

> "It will usually be appropriate to start by considering the nature of the non-compliance with the relevant rule, practice direction or court order. If this can properly be regarded as trivial, the court will usually grant relief provided that an application is made promptly. The principle "de minimis non curat lex" (the law is not concerned with trivial things) applies here as it applies in most areas of the law. Thus, the court will usually grant relief if there has been no more than an insignificant failure to comply with an order: for example, where there has been a failure of form rather than substance; or where the party has narrowly missed the deadline imposed by the order but has otherwise fully complied with its terms."

However, ask a lawyer to provide you with an explanation of what is meant by trivial and you will visibly see them shift uncomfortably and give you a traditional sitting on the fence kind of answer. A look at the cases on the issue reveals a mess, full of contradictions and a lack of consistency. The result of this splurge of satellite litigation is that an enormous amount of court time has been wasted and a new style of litigation has emerged whereby instead of working to bring the case to trial, parties are focused on catching each other out. Civil litigation has become a game of procedure rather than a fight over the substantive issues of the case.

I remember attending a seminar in London just after the decision in **Denton v TH White Ltd [2014] EWCA Civ 906**, at which the speaker was the entertaining Professor Dominic Regan. The topic of relief from sanctions came up and I posed the question that the recent increase in the court fee for applications would be a good earner for Court Service considering the strict approach taken in considering applications for relief from sanctions. I was told that I was being too cynical in my assessment but when you look back on the course of events over the last 7 years or so, perhaps my views were near the truth.

The often-draconian approach and uncertain outcomes has caused a state of panic among some lawyers and a waste of valuable court time being taken up by considering minor breaches of procedure when surely the overriding objective would be to simply get on with the current case. Now, I expect that my view on the harshness will be met by the establishment as a lack of understanding on the impact of not complying with deadlines and that a soft approach will allow lawyers to think they can be carefree about deadlines. Some may also think that I have come to my view due to missing deadlines in cases and feeling a sense of guilt like a child not being prepared to accept the punishment. Yes, I do admit to having been in a situation of needing to make an application for relief but take the view that although there is a need to ensure compliance with rules and deadlines it must be kept in proportion. The punishment does not seem to fit the crime. If the speeding motorist was 1 mph over the speed limit and the motorist was instantly banned from driving for 5 years, then you would think that was an overreaction. But it seems that in civil procedure, all common sense goes out the window and cases with merit have be sacrificed because of the strict adherence to procedure. It is bit like the "Little Britain" character who says, "The computer says no".

Lord Denning captured the reality of legal professionals

and the reasons for delays in his book "The Due Process of Law":

> *"The real reason for the delays of lawyers is not slackness or dilatoriness. They are as a class the most hardworking of all professional men. It often lies in their choice of priorities. Each case is important and must be dealt with. Each letter must be answered the same day or at any rate the next. A sudden call puts something else out of mind. The courts expect each client's case to be dealt with expeditiously."*

This comment from Denning captures the reality of legal practice. It is generally not the deliberate slowness of lawyers that causes delays. Mistakes sometimes happen when you are balancing various cases with differing priorities. You might say that it is the lawyer's fault for having too much work; having more work than you can cope with is not good practice but even if you have the right number of cases, lawyers are human and a distraction from a long telephone call can lead to something being missed.

The rules that relate to the consequences of a failure for complying with a court direction are CPR Part 3.8 and 3.9. Under CPR 3.8:

Where a party has failed to comply with a rule, practice direction or court order, any sanction for failure to comply imposed by the rule, practice direction or court order has effect unless the party in default applies for and obtains relief from the sanction.

Where there has been a failure to comply with an order, rule or practice direction, a party must make an application under CPR Part 3.9 for relief from sanctions. CPR 3.9 states:

Relief from sanctions

3.9

(1) On an application for relief from any sanction imposed for a failure to comply with any rule, practice direction or court order, the court will consider all the circumstances of the case, so as to enable it to deal justly with the application, including the need –

(a) for litigation to be conducted efficiently and at proportionate cost; and

(b) to enforce compliance with rules, practice directions and orders.

(2) An application for relief must be supported by evidence.

In **HRH Prince Abdulaziz Bin Mishal Bin Abdulaziz Al Saud v (1) Apex Global Management Ltd and another [2014] UKSC 65,** The Supreme Court clarified that the merits of the applicant's case can be considered, but only in "exceptional cases" where the merits are strong enough to obtain summary judgment.

My criticism of the strict approach to relief from sanction comes from the actual long-term effect of taking a harsh stance. In my view, if there is a continuing of this harsh approach then the only alternative is for litigants to pursue a claim for negligence against their lawyers. Not many parties would be able to commence a further action against their lawyers for negligence, and in any event, that would most likely take more court resources, which goes against the supposed purpose of enforcing compliance with Orders. It is not a certainty that such an action for professional negligence would succeed or that the party would obtain the same damages as they could have achieved in the original action.

In any event, do we really want there to be an up-surge in claims of negligence against lawyers for minor breaches of rules? I do not want to see any more of those irritating advertisements on daytime television encouraging people to bring a claim and offering "no win fees". Those types of advertisements, in my view, encourage the litigious culture. They make it appear as though whenever something goes wrong, you reach for the number of your lawyer. It is this culture which has clogged up the courts with cases and led to the introduction of "Portals" to deal with claims that are churned out by sausage factory style law firms.

The strict approach to relief from sanctions fails to take account of the real world of private legal practice and expectation of the courts that lawyers should be like some form of perfect robots that must never make mistakes.

Knee jerk reactions do not make good law. What is needed is a degree of certainty. A casual review of a series of cases applying the principle in **Denton,** would suggest that the outcome will depend on who hears your application on the day. From looking at the cases, there is a large mix of circumstances with some cases where relief is granted and others where it is not. What is obvious from this collection of cases is the vast amount of court time that has been wasted on this issue of relief from sanctions.

The established position would be that lawyers (and litigants in person) can avoid the harsh consequences by either trying to agree an extension of time with the other party or make an application to the court for an extension of time before the deadline expires. The case of **Hallam Estates v. Baker (2014) EWCA Civ 661** confirms that if you make an application before the expiry of the deadline then you are not caught within the principles of CPR Part 3.9 and Denton, even if the application is heard after the deadline.

I am advocating for a more common-sense approach and one that is consistent across all courts. A recent High Court decision demonstrates a common-sense, realistic approach to relief from sanctions. Solicitors might have become used to judges, when striking claims out, reassuring the claimant that they can always sue their solicitors for negligence. In a welcome judgment in **Badejo v Cranston [2019] EWHC 3343 (Ch)**, Mr Justice Fancourt reversed a decision to refuse relief from sanction. The claimant was seeking to recover about £120,000 that he had paid to the defendant pursuant to an option agreement. The parties were ready for trial, which was listed for 2 days in the Central London County Court. The notice of trial date required the claimant to pay a trial fee of £1,090 by a certain date or the claim would be automatically struck out. His solicitors failed to do so, and the claim was struck out. Although no explanation as to why is given in the judgment, presumably they simply forgot or mis-diarised. The claimant's solicitors applied for relief from sanction 2 days after they realised their mistake, which was 9 days after the deadline for making the payment had passed. Mr Justice Fancourt said:

23. Ultimately, in my judgment, despite the fact that a moderately serious breach was committed without mitigating circumstances, justice is better done in this case by enabling the current action to proceed to a trial, rather than requiring the appellant to start new proceedings for his claim, or alternatively a claim for negligence against the solicitors, or possibly both. Paying all the costs of the current claim, and incurring the cost of funding two new actions, would in my judgment be disproportionate to the seriousness of the breach and any harm done to the administration of justice or to the respondent that is attributable to the breach, as opposed to being attributable to the court's failure to list the application urgently. So far as prejudice to the respondent is concerned, the respondent would be equally troubled by a new claim that the appellant would be able to bring.

24. Of course in general terms defaulting litigants who have to apply for relief against sanctions may not find themselves in a position where the trial date can be saved. A busy court centre may well vacate the hearing date when it is aware that the trial fee has not been paid. In those circumstances a breach will have caused the loss of the trial date, and that will be a significant factor, as the Judge in the lower court considered it to be, in the exercise of discretion. I do not by granting relief in this case suggest that a prompt application will always be liable to result in relief being granted. In any given case, there may be circumstances that make it unjust to grant relief, particularly if the applicant has previously been in serious breach of directions or rules of the court. Litigants and solicitors are therefore well advised to take no risk with the late payment of court fees. For the reasons I have given, however, I will allow the appeal in this case, with the consequence that relief against sanctions is granted to the appellant. I will hear counsel now on the terms on which such relief should be granted.

The phrase, "*justice is better done in this case by enabling the current action to proceed to a trial, rather than requiring the appellant to start new proceedings for his claim, or alternatively a claim for negligence against the solicitors, or possibly both*", displays a common sense and realistic approach to the situation. However, how many Judges will also apply the same common-sense approach when they are under pressure from up high to make better use of scarce resources, if indeed such an approach does in the long term save court resources. The rules are too often applied harshly without a real understanding of the realities of what can sometimes happen in legal practice.

In the middle of the COVID pandemic, another judgment of common sense prevailed in the case of **Stanley v Tower Hamlets LBC [2020] EWHC 1622 (QB)** which was heard on 18 June 2020. The facts of the case were:

7. On 6 November 2019 the Claimant instructed solicitors to pursue a compensation claim. Proceedings were issued on a protective basis on 4 December 2019. The Claimant claims damages of up to £10,000. As pleaded in the Particulars of Claim, the losses claimed for are 'psychological distress, stress, inconvenience and financial loss.' These are not further particularised; there is no medical report, nor any schedule of special damages.

8. On 23 January 2020 the Claimant's solicitors sent a letter before claim to the Council by post and email. No response was received. On 6 February 2020 the Claimant's solicitors sent a second letter by post and email pointing out that the Council was in breach of the pre-action protocol (which required a response within 14 days). The Claimant's solicitor gave the Council a further seven days to respond.

9. Again, no response was received, and so on 13 February 2020 the Claimant's solicitor, Mr McConville, telephoned the Council's Legal Services Department. He was provided with the name and contact details of the file handler, who was not himself present in the office at the time; the person to whom Mr McConville spoke could not assist as it was not his case. Mr McConville told that person he would instruct counsel to draft Particulars of Claim in readiness for the service of proceedings. Mr McConville also emailed the file handler in the same terms. Mr McConville asked if the Council would accept service of proceedings by email and was told service had to be by post and that service by email would not be accepted.

This point is important in light of what happened later.

10. Particulars of Claim were drafted and signed off by counsel on or about 24 March 2020. The Council had still not replied by that date. Mr McConville put the relevant documents in the post on 25 March 2020 which meant that the deemed date of service was 27 March 2020. The Council's Acknowledgement of Service was thus due on or before 9 April 2020

Justice Julian Knowles came to the following decision on the issue of relief from sanctions:

35. I turn to the three stage Mitchell/Denton test. As I have said, Mr Cohen accepted that there had been a serious and significant default by the Council in its failure to serve an Acknowledgement of Service and a Defence. I agree. However, I accept that the circumstances which led to the default were unique and that overall I should grant relief from sanctions having regard to the second and third stages of the test and the criteria in CPR r 3.9. Here, I am bound to have regard to CPR PD 51ZA (Extension of time limits and clarification of Practice Direction 51Y – coronavirus), which provides at [4]:

> "4. In so far as compatible with the proper administration of justice, the court will take into account the impact of the COVID-19 pandemic when considering applications for the extension of time for compliance with directions, the adjournment of hearings, and applications for relief from sanctions."

36. I find that the reason for the Council's default was the COVID-19 crisis, and that, but for the Council's offices being shut, it would have responded in time to the Claimant's claim. Whilst, as I have said, the Council had shown something of a cavalier attitude prior to the issuing of proceedings, I am satisfied it would have acted in accordance with the rules once proceedings had actually been issued. Another relevant circumstance is that Mr McConville was at fault for not checking whether service by post was still possible and feasible. That was an obvious step which he should have taken. The Council moved promptly to instruct Ms McDougall once it became cognisant of the Claimant's claim and this application to set aside default judgment was made promptly thereafter. I fully recognise the need to enforce compliance with the rules and the need to conduct litigation at proportionate cost. However, overall, I am satisfied that the interests of justice require judgment in default to be set aside. It would be unconscionable in my view for the Claimant to benefit from the unprecedented health emergency which prevailed at the end of March (and which is still subsisting today).

37. I therefore set aside the judgment in default, grant relief from sanctions, and give permission to the Council to file and serve an Acknowledgment of Service and Defence. That must be done within 14 days of the date of the order giving effect to this judgment.

Although the case **of Stanley v Tower Hamlets LBC [2020] EWHC 1622 (QB)** stated that the Court will take account of the impact of COVID-19 when considering extensions of time and relief from sanctions, do not expect to succeed in such an application by simply mentioning COVID as the reason for the breach of a direction. The case of **Daly and Another v Ryan and Another [2020] EWHC 2672 (Ch**) illustrated the fact that if you rely on COVID as the excuse for breaching a direction, you will need to give a detailed explanation of how the pandemic has a caused a party to not comply with a deadline. In this case, the Application for relief from sanctions simply mentioned the pandemic and the Defendant having to isolate.

SUMMARY

I have stated that I favour the courts taking a more sensible approach to relief from sanctions applications. A way to achieve a common-sense approach is to have consistency in decisions. Courts should resist the temptation to be too draconian when considering applications for relief from sanctions. Justice is not served by determining cases by minor breaches in procedure. The courts should recognise that even lawyers are human, and mistakes are made. It is ironic that if a court makes a mistake in its administration, there are few consequences. Punishing litigants too harshly for breaches of procedure will simply lead to more cases arriving through another door, most likely that of professional negligence. So overall, it does not save court resources but creates other cases in different areas.

Chapter 8

The Impact on Lawyers and their Clients

The onset of the COVID pandemic in March 2020 led to the Prime Minister urging people to work from home where possible. Law firms up and down the country rushed to set up remote working so that the businesses could continue to function. Courts continued to operate as best they could but many in-person cases were adjourned and as many as possible switched to a remote hearing, such as by video link or by telephone. What this chapter explores is that the greater switch to home and remote working that was accelerated by COVID, will likely lead to a change in the structure of law firms; this change could benefit the client by tempering the extreme fees that exist in some areas of the legal market.

The change to total home working would have been a strange new experience for many lawyers. Although working from home on an occasional basis is not something that would have been totally alien, not being able to see clients on a face-to-face basis was a new experience. Obviously, certain types of law can be managed fine remotely but not in every situation. There are certain benefits in being able to meet face-to-face with a client or a witness. In litigation, the way witness statements have been obtained has become more scrutinised. There have been many comments in cases relating to poorly prepared witness statements in the Business & Property Courts so a new Practice Direction was introduced on 6 April 2021 requiring statements to have a certificate of compliance to confirm the statement has been prepared in accordance with best practice. This new practice direction is a very welcome development as I am amazed by some of the witness statements that are prepared for the trial. Many appear like skeleton arguments prepared by lawyers. This has arisen by either the fact that the lawyer was not adept at taking statements or had a very dominant client who demanded certain things go in their statements; with dominant clients, the lawyers may decide to give in and put the information in their statement (knowing it is not appropriate) to simply avoid a complaint from the client.

To prepare a witness statement that complies with the Civil Procedure Rules and Practice Directions, there will need to be an interview with the client. Does this always have to be in person? To some lawyers, the thought of more client contact fills them with dread. Having a face-to-face meeting with a client usually contains all those irritating pleasantries, having to make inane conversation as you walk with the client from the reception area to an interview room or your office. This will sound like I do not like client contact; that is not the case. I prefer client contact on the telephone. Having a meeting with a client on the telephone or by video link, saves time as it leaves out all the time wasted on walking to your office and the small talk that goes with it. Also, the

THE IMPACT ON LAWYERS AND THEIR CLIENTS

client is less nervous if they are sat at home on the telephone or on a video link. A client who had a stressful car journey or braved the daily squash on the train, may not be in the best frame of mind when they arrive at the lawyer's office. If a client is at home or in their office talking to you by telephone or a video link, they are more likely to have access to all the documents they need for the meeting and so avoiding that annoying situation where the client says they have not brought the crucial papers.

Working remotely is so much easier with the advent of modern technology. Gone are the days when a client's files are retained solely in paper form. The old traditional High Street practice often had large storerooms set aside to retain the papers or hired outside storage facilities to house old files. Client correspondence and documents are now usually held in electronic form in the cloud enabling the lawyer to access a case from anywhere. The Regulatory bodies rightly keep an eye on the safety of data in these situations, but if sensible precautions are taken and you work with trustworthy providers, that should ensure the client's information is not compromised. Using a predominantly paperless office means that those working from home should not have large bundles of client documents lying around at home. Where there is a need to print off documents to work on, the confidentially of the client can easily be maintained by shredding these papers after use. There might be other concerns about client confidentiality when working from home or away from the office. During the COVID lockdown, there would likely be others around at home and you would not want the children nosing into client documents or overhearing confidential conversations on the telephone or by video link. Conducting court hearings requires a quiet environment where you do not want your key submission to the judge to be interrupted by your neighbour's lawnmower. These issues can be dealt with by a bit of sensible planning and having a dedicated room at home which is used as an office rather than working from the kitchen table in front of daytime television.

Not only do Regulatory bodies worry about data protection, but they like to know that proper supervision of staff working remotely is happening. Having fee earners working remotely with all the client files held in a centralised cloud is an easier way to ensure supervision takes place. The supervising lawyers can easily be given access to files of the fee earners they are supervising to ensure that professional practice is being followed.

Did the COVID pandemic really highlight the fact that the small High Street practice, where you drop in to see your local solicitor who turns his hand to most legal problems, was a dying breed? In fact, there has been a move for a long time away from this type of legal firm. The reason for the decline in the small local High Street firm was consumer led as people wanted cheaper legal services. The way to provide these cheaper services was to develop the sausage factory style firm that churns out a large amount of a particular area of work, such as conveyancing or personal injury claims. Invariably, these firms will consist of a large department of para-legals who work under the supervision of a few solicitors. This sort of bulk production with fewer qualified lawyers enables the service to be provided at a lower cost. In my view, that is fine if your case is a straightforward "transaction" and there is little actual law involved and you do not mind the lack of personal contact. However, these firms, I would argue,

THE IMPACT ON LAWYERS AND THEIR CLIENTS

do not appeal to clients who have a case that does not fit a familiar pattern or scenario.

If you are only paying what in legal terms would be considered a "cheap fee" your case is not getting the in-depth consideration that it might otherwise get. That may be fine if you are doing a bog-standard conveyancing transaction or a simple personal injury claim, but when a case throws up something unusual or takes an unexpected turn, there is potential danger ahead. That is the point where the more experienced supervising lawyer should step in and address the issue. However, the problem is that the less qualified fee earner will not always pick up on the problem that is fast approaching and only when something goes wrong does the supervisor pick up the file and try a rescue mission. In conveyancing that might lead to a delay, which whilst annoying may not be fatal, but in other areas of the law such as litigation it could lead to the claim/defence collapsing because it has been struck out for a failure to comply with case management directions. With the courts taking a tough line on a failure to comply with deadlines and other court directions, you cannot always expect to get out of jail with a simple application for relief from sanctions. However, I would imagine that these large firms with such a business model expect such scenarios to be relatively few and that the larger turnover they create can cope with these disasters. Even if that does knock their PI premiums, they would take the overall view that the profits generated by this type of legal organisation can cope with it. It is perhaps not too concerned by the damaged client relationship because there is a large turnover of cases, there are not so many repeat clients and therefore less client loyalty, as the clients in this model are simply seeking the cheapest provider at that time.

The client will expect the same level of professional service no matter who is dealing with the case and no matter what fee is being paid. It is not a defence to a negligence claim for the lawyer to turn around and say, "I did not know what I was doing/you were not paying enough for the firm to take proper care of your case". However, in my view, the consumer ought to know that you get what you pay for. As the public over the years mocked what were regarded as excessive legal fees, this led to the creation of sausage factories to be able to take advantage of economies of scale, but the expectation of what you get for paying peanuts is unrealistic.

In my view, the COVID pandemic will hasten a move to the development of small law firms that are able to provide more reasonable fees than the traditional high street practice and the large commercial city firms. They may not be able to match the fees of the sausage factories but the ability to offer the lower fees will stem from an increase in virtual firms which do not have the overheads of a firm that has to finance large plush offices for all its lawyers.

There is a wide mix of law firms and lawyers in England and Wales. Prior to the advent of COVID in March 2020, the number of lawyers working fully from home was not at the level that exists now. That is not to say that every lawyer was sat in those ivory towers in a city or a large provincial town. The past decade has seen an increase in the use by law firms of "consultants". Consultant lawyers are self-employed and work as and when the work comes in and can decide whether to take on a case or not. This is different to an employee, who would be expected to take on the work that is put their way.

Many of these consultants are lawyers with a fair degree of experience and are seeking a different balance between work and home life. They will often work remotely from home, but to the outside world and the client, they are part of the law firm. Many consultants will work for different firms at the same time.

The use of self-employed consultants has benefits to the firm and to the consultant. It gives the firm more flexibility because it does not need to employ as many lawyers. If there is a big upturn in work, they can utilise more consultants. When there is a downturn in work, they do not have to pay them which they would if they wanted to keep employees on the payroll. The law firm benefits from the lower costs incurred using consultants as they come without the expense of employing permanent staff.

The lawyer will be covered by the firm's professional indemnity insurance and will usually be paid by taking a percentage of the fees that are received.

The advantage to the consultant is they can take on as much or as little work as they want, although some firms would like consultants to be able to provide a certain number of days. Consultants generally tend to be lawyers who have more experience and are at the end of their careers. They usually have specialist knowledge and will probably be utilised in the more unusual and complex cases.

The law firm that utilises consultants in the way described above, will often be virtual firms in that, apart from one administrative office that deals with post and other admin, they will probably not have other offices as most of the work is done remotely by consultants. If a client needs to be seen in person, either the lawyer will go to visit the client, or a meeting room will be booked at a convenient place for the client.

These types of "virtual law firms" were able to adapt more easily to the impact of the COVID lockdown. They already had processes in place that enabled work to be done remotely and the imposition of lockdown had no real impact on how and where the work was done. Obviously, COVID has had an impact on the amount of work as people have not been able to afford to instruct lawyers, but these virtual firms were best able to manage the storm because their overheads were already lower and would be able to continue to provide the same level of service as before.

I see the growth of these virtual firms as a way of bringing expertise to clients at a more reasonable price. The big city firms charge fees that make your eyes water. We often assume that with costs comes quality. But when it comes to legal services, cost is not always an indicator of quality. In the City, top notch law firms charge high hourly rates which their clients rarely seem to question. The large fees are generated by the huge entourage of lawyers that come when instructing such a firm. The bill covers not only the fee of the lawyer but the overheads of the firm. Naturally, most reasonable consumers would be fine with this – if the overheads were essential in delivering the high-quality service they received. City law firms have outlandish overheads. They operate from some of the choicest locations where rent is sky high. As well as office space, your bill covers the cost of assistants, juniors, paralegals, and legal secretaries. In addition, there is the cost of professional indemnity insurance and regulatory requirements.

There was undoubtedly a move towards remote working

before COVID, but it has certainly accelerated this shift. Remote working does rely heavily on modern information technology and the client files being stored and accessed on-line. The use of information technology in the business world and the professions was moving this way anyway and the COVID shutdown was an event that would mean there would probably never be the same need for office structure as before. Law firms will still need some form of office presence, but I see that being mainly for the receipt of post and for when a meeting needs to take place face to face.

I have already questioned why large city firms saw the need to have large and plush buildings. To me it is all about image and status. I remember going to a meeting at a large firm in London to discuss a case. I attended with our Counsel and we met with the partner in charge of the case and a more junior solicitor who was assisting. We waited in the large modern reception area surrounded by large glass windows from floor to ceiling. Eventually we were shown up to an office on some high up floor. The room had a very minimal feel about it with little office furniture apart from a big desk at the end of the room behind which they sat. What was noticeable was how the desk and their chairs were on a raised platform, so that when we sat opposite them on more basic chairs it was obvious that they looked down on us. To me, such psychological games meant nothing, I do recall, however, we went on to obtain an excellent settlement for our clients.

Image is everything to some large law firms. They have developed their brand, probably taking over many smaller firms, and believe that helps them achieve success. In my view, this is a myth that has been peddled by larger firms that like to create the impression to clients (and their opponents in litigation) that size and status equals success. On many occasions, I have experienced larger firms treating small firms as something you have just scraped off your shoe when walking your dog. They use such tactics to make more timid lawyers run scared of a big fight and so hopefully come begging for a settlement. Thankfully, we have an excellent judiciary who look at the case on its merits and apply the law; the law does not change just because you employed big expensive lawyers; it might be that they will have greater resources to present the case in a more flash and aggressive way, but at the end of the day, if you comply with the court rules and practice directions when taking your case to trial, the judges are not going to be influenced by the size and status of the firm representing the client.

Some people will say that the rich get the result they achieve because they have access to large expensive lawyers, but it would be interesting to see whether on the evidence that is correct. What is crucial is that you employ a lawyer who understands the issue and the law and instruct a competent Counsel to present the case at trial. The key to selecting lawyers should be their skill and knowledge of the case rather than the status and size of the firm they work for. Now it is often the case that larger firms will employ the more skilled lawyers in their field because they can afford to pay them the bigger rewards that a specialist is entitled to demand. But it does not necessarily follow that you do not find experts working in different types of organisations. For the client, it will be a matter of choice as to who they work with best. That is often a key to a good lawyer/client relationship. Clients like to feel comfortable with the person

THE IMPACT ON LAWYERS AND THEIR CLIENTS

who is representing them, and they like to have that personal contact. Clients also realise that the personal contact does not always happen when instructing a large firm. The more senior lawyers in bigger firms seem to spend an inordinate amount of time in meetings and discussing ways to market the business; this of course will be done in conjunction with the larger marketing department. Does a successful or likeable lawyer really need a big marketing department?

The move away from the large law firms which are like the old "super groups" of the progressive rock era in the 1970's (when some musicians did things to excess) could be curtailed if the Regulatory regime gets concerned by the change in their income stream. The Solicitors Regulation

Firms Annual Periodic Fees

Turnover Band (T)	Turnover Range (A)	Pay % of turnover within Band (B)	Minimum Turnover in Band (C)	Minimum Fee in Band (D)
A	£0–19,999	0.69%	£0	£100
B	£20–£149,999	0.41%	£20,000	£239
C	£150–£499,999	0.39%	£150,000	£272
D	£500–£999,999	0.38%	£500,000	£2,137
E	£1,000,000 £2,999,999	0.36%	£1,000,000	£4,037
F	£3,000,000 £9,999,999	0.25%	£3,000,000	£11,237
G	£10,000,000 £29,999,999	0.21%	£10,000,000	£28,737
H	£30,000,000 £69,999,999	0.19%	£30,000,000	£70,737
I	£70,000,000 £149,999,999	0.17%	£70,000,000	£145,737

Source: SRA website: www.sra.org.uk/mysra/fees/current-fees/

Authority ("SRA") may get nervous if there is a shift away to smaller firms with lower turnover. In addition to the individual solicitor having to pay a practicing fee of £338 per annum, the solicitors' firm must pay an annual periodic fee calculated by a percentage of their turnover.

The periodic fee is calculated using the above table and the formula: Fee = (T − C) x B + D. A small firm with a turnover of £200,000 would pay:

(£200,000 − £150,000) x 0.39 + £772 = £967

A firm with a turnover of £279,123,528 would pay:

(£279,123,528 − £150,000,000) x 0.06 + £282,737 = £360,211

SUMMARY

It will always be the case that there are "horses for courses" when it comes to selecting the type of law firm to take on your case. The type of firm a client instructs will depend on several factors such as the expertise required in a particular matter, their fees and who the client feels comfortable working with. What I believe COVID will hasten is the shift away from large law firms occupying plush city buildings and charging hourly rates that make a night at the Ritz seem cheap. I believe more lawyers will see the benefit of smaller and more personalised firms working remotely or in smaller offices, who are able to provide the same heavyweight litigation services but at much more reasonable fees.

Chapter 9

Funding the Civil Courts

Perhaps the major problem facing the Civil Courts after COVID will be how to fund them without closing access to those who need them. The approach of successive Governments since 2002 has been to increase the amount of funding that comes from court fees. The objective since then has been to try to make the Civil Courts self-funding. The inevitable result of that has been a massive increase in court fees, well above the actual cost of the work done and inflation. At the time of writing this chapter, the Court Service announced another consultation on a further increase to some civil fees. It is the first increase since 2016 and the proposed fee rises do not seem as high as one might have expected. However, when you look at the existing level of some fees, any increase in fees will cause hardship to those struggling to fund legal action. Rather than simply shout outrage whenever fees are increased, there needs to be a debate about how the civil justice system is funded in the long term. Without proper analysis of its funding, the civil courts (especially at County Court level) will continue to limp along, providing an inadequate service to those fortunate enough to be able to afford legal action.

Since the objective of making courts largely self-funding, not only has this led to big fee increases but also a policy of driving people away from using the courts, applying strong pressure to utilise alternatives such as mediation. It is probably true that the imposition of higher court fees has persuaded many to not take court action. Successive Governments have taken to restricting the spending on the civil courts, including selling off court buildings and reducing the amount of sitting days by Judges. Also, the number of admin staff has been reduced by a third. In the background, there have been moves to increase on-line courts but the expected going-live dates for this new technology keeps getting pushed back and there are doubts about whether it will work. To some, this could be another Government technology project that never sees the light of day and wastes a load of public money.

As the new Court Fee increases were announced in March 2021, it was revealed that the cost of running the Courts and Tribunal Service was £2 billion a year; court fees raised £724 million in 2019/20.[4] That may seem a lot of money to provide justice but when you consider that the announced changes to the overseas aid budget would bring savings of £4 billion, it is in my view a question of reallocating priorities. Some of the monies that would have been spent on foreign aid could be spent on the civil justice system. This may be a controversial view to those who exploded with indignation when a reduction in the percentage of GDP to be spent on foreign aid was announced. However, it is my view that having a properly funded justice system is a higher priority

---

[4] The Law Society Gazette, 26 March 2021.

than foreign aid. No doubt the opponents of my suggestion will say that other ways should be found to fund the court service. My question to them is what other way is as effective as having the court service regarded as a fundamental public service, such as the NHS, and being fully funded by the taxpayer?

Are there other ways of funding the civil justice service which is compatible with its primary objective to deliver justice to those who need it irrespective of their financial means? Having the civil courts so heavily reliant on court fees is not producing fair results. An overseas rich businessperson or a large multi-national company can use the High Court in London to resolve a high value dispute by paying what to them is a mere £10,000 to commence legal action. To others that puts court action out of reach. Undoubtedly there are those who will find ways to raise the money to commence action, through legal expenses insurance or through crowd funding, but high court fees leave many ordinary citizens or small businesses without recourse to civil justice. I am sure that in many cases, the defendants take advantage of knowing that the Claimant (who has a good case) will not issue court action because of the high court fees. I have noticed in recent times, there are lot more threats of legal action being made but not being followed through. Now there could be other reasons but the generally higher court fees are anecdotally having an impact on whether to pursue a legitimate case. The continuing rise in court fees will cause a reduction in the cases issued and also a reduction in the amount collected in fees, and that will be used by the Government to further increase fees or to make additional cuts to the virtually non-existent admin staff.

When you consider objectively the options for funding the civil courts, there are several options, some of which are controversial. The possibilities include:

1. Higher Government public spending
2. High Court fees
3. Higher court fees on those who can afford it by way of means testing the court user.
4. Introducing more court fees, such as re-introducing court fees for employment tribunal claims.
5. The introduction of a "court fee levy" on large law firms with annual revenue over a certain amount.

The first option of high public spending on the civil courts is not a political priority despite the moral arguments for it. Higher court fees (as has been mentioned above) has not produced fair results and reduces the access to justice for the less well off in society. However, the Government will say that the level for qualifying for a fee remission has increased, but only by a small amount. The threshold for help with court fees will be £1,165 per month for a single person and £1,355 for a couple when changes take place in the autumn of 2021. It is therefore apparent that you must have little in the way of savings as well as a low gross monthly income. The test for fee remission is summarised below:

The Disposable Capital Test
A party satisfies the disposable capital test if–

1. the fee for which an application for remission is made, falls within a fee band set out in column 1 of the "Disposable Capital Threshold Table" below; and

2. the party's disposable capital is less than the amount in the corresponding row of column 2.

Disposable Capital Threshold Table

Court / Tribunal Fee	Disposable capital
Up to/ including £1,000	£ 3,000
£ 1,001 to £ 1,335	£ 4,000
£ 1,336 to £ 1,665	£ 5,000
£ 1,666 to £ 2,000	£ 6,000
£ 2,001 to £ 2,330	£ 7,000
£ 2,331 to £ 4,000	£ 8,000
£ 4,001 to £ 5,000	£ 10,000
£ 5,001 to £ 6,000	£ 12,000
£ 6,001 to £ 7,000	£ 14,000
£ 7,001 or more	£ 16,000

Gross Monthly Income Test

If you have passed the "Disposable Capital Test" you may be entitled to a full or part remission.

Benefits

If you are in receipt of any of the following benefits you may be entitled to a full remission:

1. Income-based Jobseeker's Allowance
2. Income-related Employment and Support Allowance
3. Income Support

4. Universal Credit with gross annual earnings of less than £ 6,000
5. State Pension Credit guarantee credit
6. Scottish Civil Legal Aid (not Advice and Assistance or Advice by Way of Representation)

Income Threshold Table

If your gross monthly income is between the minimum income threshold and the maximum income cap, you may be eligible for a partial remission.

Minimum Income Threshold	Maximum Income Cap
£1,085	£5,085

In addition, for each child add £ 245 and if you are part of a couple £160. For every £10 of income you have over the threshold, you will be required to pay £ 5 towards your fee.

To give an example of non-eligibility, if you are a single person and you are needing to pay a court fee of £1,000 to start a claim for £20,000 (issue fee being 5% of the Claim if issued through County Court Money Claims Centre) with modest savings of £3,100 and a gross monthly income of £2,075, you would not be entitled to a fee remission. To put this in perspective, The Office of National Statistics released figures in December 2020 showing the average salary for over 400 job roles (from gardeners to artists, IT technicians to sales and marketing managers) in the UK for men and women combined was £29,009, which includes those in both full-time and part work. In my example above, the gross salary of the person seeking a fee remission is £24,907 per annum, being the starting salary of a newly qualified nurse in 2021. It might be optimistic to assume that a newly qualified nurse would have savings of £3,100. So, if we assume that the person had no saving at all, then the person would still be expected to pay £490 of the £1,000 court fee.

The introduction of more court fees to certain tribunals, such as the Employment Tribunal, would not be popular or indeed fair as most people claiming a remedy to such a Tribunal may not be in employment.

A more controversial proposal to improve funding of the Civil Courts would be to impose a lawyer levy on larger law firms whose revenue exceeds a certain level. A proposal of this nature was put forward by Michael Gove in 2015 (when he was Lord Chancellor) to pay for legal aid.[5] Leading law firms were heavily critical of this proposal saying that they already invested large sums in *pro-bono* work. When you look at the revenues of the leading law firms in figures produced by "The Lawyer", I am inclined to think this option needs serious consideration. The insurance industry must pay a levy to fund the Motor Insurance Bureau ("MIB")[6] and therefore I do not believe this suggestion is so outlandish. These leading firms are those who are benefitting most from using the system and its clients are more than likely wealthy individuals or large organisations who could afford to contribute more to the running of the civil courts.

Large law firms who say that it is unfair because they already contribute to *pro-bono* services, in my view misses

---

[5] The Guardian, 23 June 2015.
[6] The Motor Insurers' Bureau (MIB) was founded in the UK in 1946 and is the mechanism in the UK through which compensation is provided for victims of accidents caused by uninsured and untraced drivers, which is funded by a levy on every insured driver's premium.

the point. The levy in this proposal would go to assist the running of the Court. Without the money to run a Court system, there would be little point in providing *pro-bono* services if those in need of the advice do not have Courts to enforce their rights. It all sounds great to have advice to say that your legal rights are "X" or "Y", but those against whom you are trying to seek redress do not simply roll over if you tell them that you have certain legal rights. Many large organisations have the resources to put obstacles in the way and make you fight to achieve what you are entitled to.

Even with greater funding from the Government and a levy on large law firms turning over a certain level of revenue, there will still be the need for some court fees. Without court fees, it leaves the court open to more vexatious litigation from parties who issue excessive applications and claims which have no merit. Having a certain level of court fee contributes a certain degree of deterrence. Court fees were introduced for Employment Tribunal fees in 2013. The Supreme Court ruled in 2017 that the Tribunal fees were unlawful. A summary of the decision is set out below.

R (Unison) v Lord Chancellor [2017] UKSC 51

The Supreme Court unanimously ruled that the employment tribunal fee regime in place since 2013 was unlawful. It stressed the importance of the rule of law. Inherent in that is a UK constitutional right of access to the courts. 'Without such access, laws are liable to become a dead letter, the work done by Parliament may be rendered nugatory, and the democratic election of Members of Parliament may become a meaningless charade'. The Supreme Court made clear that access to tribunals and other courts provides a service to society in general rather than just to individual claimants: for example, resolving unclear issues of law, and society being aware that there is a remedy if legal rights are breached.

Accordingly, in the absence of clear authority in the relevant Act of Parliament, the Lord Chancellor cannot impose fees if there is a real risk that persons will effectively be prevented from having access to justice, and the degree of intrusion must not be greater than is justified by the objectives which the measure is intended to serve. The court held that the current fee regime did not meet either of these tests. The court pointed for example to the long-term reduction of around 66-70% in claims accepted by tribunals. It said fees must be reasonably affordable, not just affordable in a theoretical sense. Also, rather than the fees deterring unmeritorious claims as intended there was now a larger proportion of unsuccessful claims; the fees had not encouraged settlement of claims as was intended, indeed they could deter employers from settling as employers waited to see whether the claimant would pay the fees; and it was elementary economics that maximising the fees was not the way to maximise government revenue from them, given their deterrent effect.

In my experience, from having handled Employment Law claims prior to the introduction of Tribunal Fees in 2013, it was clear that there were many claims which had dubious merits. Many law firms were offering "contingency fees" where the lawyer charges a percentage of damages recovered. This is not the same as a "conditional fee agreement" (no win no fee agreements) where fees become due upon a successful outcome. The legal representatives would take on a case in the hope that the employer would throw some money to settle the claim rather than spend the time and costs of defending it. As there is a general no costs rule in employment tribunals, it made economic sense to offer at an early stage a figure of say £5,000 to make the claim go away. An early settlement meant the Claimant's lawyer had not done too much work and a 20% to 25% fee of £5,000 provided a reasonable return for the lawyer and an acceptable level of compensation for the client without having to take any risk. This was the mischief which tribunal fees were designed to tackle and thus reduce the number of claims.

Although the Supreme Court decision ruled the fee regime in 2013 was unlawful, it does not mean that any employment tribunal fees will be unlawful. The government could pass regulations introducing a new system of fees which are more proportionate and affordable, and which do not have such a deterrent effect on people enforcing their legal rights.

SUMMARY

The funding of the Civil Justice system is something that needs to be addressed urgently before the whole system degenerates into a mess. Without intervention, what will be left is a system that will only work in parts and usually for those who can afford it. Properly funded and efficient civil courts across the board from County Court to the Higher Courts of Appeal are needed in a modern and just society. Higher court fees are currently seen as the only way to raise funding. I have suggested one alternative, which is controversial to the legal profession, but is an example of thinking more creatively to raise the necessary funds. A levy on large law firms that have high turnovers is worth exploring. They are court users and having better funded and more efficient courts would ultimately benefit them and their clients. It seems a more just way of sharing the burden of funding the system rather than ever increasing court fees which lead to the exclusion of those who cannot afford court fees.

Conclusion

Before the onset of the first wave of COVID in March 2020, the civil courts were trundling along in their normal way, especially the County Courts. With the realisation that many courts would need to be conducted remotely, there was an impressive wake up and the civil courts quickly switched many important trials to an online hearing. It was encouraging to see how, when faced with a major global pandemic, the courts were able to quickly adapt and keep the court service operating. There were of course some issues at the beginning, with many cases being adjourned, but a few months into the COVID pandemic, Nightingale Courts were established in some areas to address backlogs. Not all court had the available technology, but much greater use of technology was made, and the court system continued to function.

Whilst court hearings continued, the back administration services were affected, and Orders and other documents were not being produced as quickly as before.

The reaction of the Ministry of Justice to the pandemic illustrated that faced with a crisis, plans can be put into action to deal with threats to the operation of justice. If the court service can react constructively to problems posed by COVID, then it should also be able to react to the underlying problems in the civil courts which include:

- Under-funding
- Court closures
- Lack of court administration staff
- Lack of judges
- The simplification and removal of unnecessary civil procedure rules and processes such as costs budgeting

COVID will bring a change in the work patterns across the country, with an increase in remote working which was starting to appear before the pandemic. The civil court should continue as far as possible to use remote hearings for shorter applications and hearings. This change in work patterns brought about by COVID will also impact on the nature of law firms with a move away to smaller ones that provide a more personal service working from remote offices; these firms will place less importance on having a big city presence. This should benefit the consumer as it presents an opportunity to provide specialist advice at more reasonable fees.

Anthony Reeves
May 2021

Index

Administrative staff, 3
Alternative Dispute Resolution, 27, 40
Arbitration, 87

Barristers, 30
Business & Property Courts, 114

Case Management Conference, 58, 59
Central London County Court, 7, 20
Civil Courts, 20, 125
Civil Procedure Rules, 1, 34, 40, 41, 50, 77, 97
Civil justice system, 1, 2, 16
Consultants, 119
Costs budgeting, 3, 17, 27, 29, 31, 32, 34, 37, 41, 92
Costs and Case Management Conference, 30
Cost churning, 18
CPR Part 27, 25
County Court Money Claims Centre, 14, 20
Court fees, 16, 23, 64, 126

Courts and Tribunal Service, 31
COVID, 2, 3, 7, 10, 17, 19, 20, 26, 28, 29, 63, 64, 65,66, 72, 110, 113, 116, 118, 120, 125, 137

Directions Questionnaire, 26, 89
Disclosure, 27, 55, 61
Disclosure Pilot Scheme 2019, 56
Disposable Capital Test, 129

E-filing, 6, 22, 23
Employment Law, 133
Employment Tribunal, 131, 132
Estimated costs, 30
Extended Court Hours, 80
Extended Disclosure, 58

Fast-track, 25, 95
Fixed recoverable legal costs, 4
Funding the Civil Courts, 125
High Court, 5, 6, 17, 19, 22, 23, 75
High Court fees, 23

Incurred costs, 20

Initial Disclosure, 58
Inspection, 27

Law Society Gazette, 29, 39
Law Society, 37
Listing in County Courts, 12
Litigants, 75

Magistrates Courts, 17
Mediation, 27
Middle-track, 91
Ministry of Justice, 2, 16, 40, 95, 137
Money-Claims-Online, 19, 20, 22, 77
Motor Insurance Bureau, 131
Multi-track, 27, 91, 92

Nightingale Courts, 17, 137

Online filing, 76

Palm tree justice, 59, 60
Pandemic, 3
Paperless office, 115
Pre-Action Practice Direction, 49
Pre-Action Protocol for Debt Claims, 47

Pre-trial review, 27

Relief from sanctions, 3, 100, 111
Remote hearings, 70, 85

Skype, 66
Small claims track, 59, 76, 84, 86, 89

Teams, 66
Telephone hearings, 7, 63
The Court Service, 2
The Solicitors Regulation Authority, 123
The Supreme Court, 132, 134

Upper-track, 92, 93

Video Hearings Process Evaluation (Phase 2) 2020, 64
Video trials, 64, 70

Witness Statements, 27, 67
Woolf Reforms of 1999, 10, 16, 40, 41, 45

Zoom, 66

Further books in the Emerald Guides Series

A STRAIGHTFORWARD GUIDE TO BAILIFF LAW –
A GUIDE FOR CREDITORS AND DEBTORS

By Anthony Reeves

ISBN 978-1-846716-595-4

HOW TO BE A LITIGANT IN PERSON
IN THE NEW LEGAL WORLD

By Michael Langford

978-1-84716-716-3